How to

HIRE + MANAGE

Market
Research
Agencies

Kathryn Korostoff

Published by Research RockStar LLC
Box 394
290 Turnpike Road, Suite 6
Westborough, MA 01581

Design: Jakdesign, New York City

The author and publisher assume no responsibility for errors and ommissions within this book. Neither the author nor the publisher is in the business of rendering legal or accounting advice. If such advice is desired, proper experts should be sought.

Special discounts on bulk quantities of this book are available to corporations, professional associations, and other organizations. For details, contact Sales, Research RockStar LLC, Box 394, 290 Turnpike Road, Suite 6, Westborough, MA 01581, or sales@researchrockstar.com.

ISBN: 978-0-615-27114-9

ACKNOWLEDGEMENTS

Thanks to the hundreds of fantastic clients I have had the pleasure to work with over the years. It's from my actual, real-world client experiences that I found myself with a mental inventory of best practices that made this book possible.

Several friends took the time to read my manuscript and provide feedback. Thanks to Alan Greenberg (my long time research comrade), Steve Hoch (research client extraordinaire), Kimberly Horning (research guru), Chris Neal (high tech research guru), Rick Pollack (statistician supreme), Alex Rassey (marketing maverick), and Jenn Wrubel (research manager wizard).

For making me look good, I must credit the team at Jak Design which endured working with me on this book's cover art and interior layout.

And a special thank you to my daughter Monica for her inspiring exuberance, and my VH, Steve, for everything.

Table of Contents

Why another book about market research?

If you search on the Internet, you'll see plenty of market research (MR) books. But on closer examination, most are targeted at two specific categories of readers: (1) professional market researchers who are seeking to advance their skills, and (2) do-it-yourself (DIY) market researchers—often people within a corporate marketing department who want to conduct MR on a very small budget and without the help of an outside MR agency. Sure, those are important groups—but they are not the only audiences who need MR information.

For this book, the intended audience is different.

This book is for people who are actual buyers and users of custom MR; those who hire and manage MR agencies and are seeking to optimize the process, minimize the risk, and improve the actionability of end results. Typically, these are people who need precise, concise, practical information to make sure that they can hit the ground running. So, if you are in any of the following situations, this book will be a useful resource:

- You have never done custom MR before, and you've been tasked with hiring and managing a research agency for the first time.

- You have previously hired MR agencies and been dissatisfied with the results.

- You have managed one or two projects with MR agency partners, but the results were not embraced by your internal clients/stakeholders.

In addition to the need for information geared toward these scenarios, I have a few observations about the limitations of many existing MR books:

- Many books lack coverage of fundamental MR challenges and short-comings. Look, I'm a professional market researcher and am enthusiastic about its benefits. But I also feel it is best to be brutally honest about its risks and limitations. There are a lot of moving parts in MR. It's part art and part science. And, alas, it's all complex.

- Many current MR books offer very high-level information that, in my opinion, is very theoretical. Such books make it hard for readers to sift out the grains of truly useful information they can apply to real-world situations.

- Many books are simply out of date given current context. MR has gone through a lot of change in the past three years. Yes, the traditional methods still apply. In the world of MR, we still use a lot of questionnaires, focus groups, in-depth interviews, and now online surveys and focus groups. Today, however, we have more robust DIY options, significant respondent quality issues, and a shifting landscape of MR suppliers. We're at a very particular (even peculiar) time in the world of MR, both in terms of what is possible and what methods are going to yield good results.

Market Research: An Industry Beleaguered?

Currently, the single greatest challenge is sample quality. It's harder and harder to find qualified people who comply with our requests to participate in research. Why? Well, there are a lot of reasons—some specific to business-to-business (B2B) research and others to business-to-consumer (B2C) research. One of my pet peeves in this area is the aggressive solicitation of MR participants by some of the panel companies (companies that pre-recruit and manage groups of willing research participants).

Unfortunately, there are many websites that randomly recruit people to take MR surveys for money. Their pitch? "Earn money easily." It is true that it's a convention in the MR industry to pay people perhaps $5, $10, or $20 to complete a survey. We have always felt in the industry that it's important to thank qualified people for their time. Not surprisingly, it does help with response rates.

There is a difference, though, between thanking qualified respondents who participate in research and dangling the carrot of easy money in front of the broad population. Unfortunately, there are people doing business on the Internet who have decided that they should promote research participation as a way to make easy money, not necessarily keeping the validity of the MR responses in mind. I believe this is one reason we have seen a decline in respondent quality.

MAXIMIZE SUCCESS: KNOW THE RISKS

MR can be very challenging. There are many risks, but if it's planned properly and executed precisely, and if the results are presented such that people can digest and apply them, it can be a very important tool in the business-planning tool chest.

I'm a big believer in preemptive strikes as a way to minimize the risks associated with market research, and much of this book's content describes and recommends these possible actions. But the first step is awareness of the risks you are likely to face. Armed with knowledge of common roadblocks, the chance of success increases. Table 1.1 displays the 12 most common factors that contribute to the failure of a MR project.

TABLE 1.1 Top 12 Reasons MR Projects Fail

Objectives are unclear, leading to conflicting or unrealistic expectations.
This often is due to imprecise or too many goals.
RESULT: muddy research, weak data.

Sample has quality issues (participants are not sufficiently qualified or authenticated, or do not pay adequate attention), or needed sample size is unmet.
RESULT: weak data, insufficient data (sample too small for use in extrapolation), research loses credibility.

Instrument is poorly designed. Long, complicated questionnaire design (or rambling discussion guides for focus groups or in-depth interviews) confuses participants with awkward question sequences and poor answer options.
RESULT FOR QUANTITATIVE: low response rates, high dropout rates, respondent fatigue, pencil whipping, weak data.
RESULT FOR QUALITATIVE: muddy, biased interviews or focus groups; disengaged participants.

Data analysis is conducted with more attention to techniques than results; either the choice of analytics is poor or is misaligned with client needs.
RESULT: misleading data, low usefulness.

Poor matching of methodology to goals and audience needs (incorrect use of qualitative or quantitative methods).
RESULT: misleading data, low usefulness.

Schedules slip significantly; research is completed too late to support intended decisions.
RESULT: research loses credibility, agency loses credibility.

Internal skeptics or cynics derail the final presentation.
RESULT: research loses credibility.

Internal clients unable to apply the research as originally intended; "actionability" of research is called into question.
RESULT: research is "shelved," research loses credibility.

Research firm's representatives are unable to establish required level of credibility with client or internal clients.
RESULT: research is "shelved," research loses credibility, agency loses credibility.

Programming (for online or telephone data collection) is done hastily, and questionnaire logic is not enforced nor approved by client. Entire questions are missing, and answer options are not properly presented.
RESULT: incomplete data, research loses credibility, agency loses credibility.

Research report contains egregious errors.
RESULT: research is "shelved," research loses credibility, agency loses credibility.

Client-agency relationship is unproductive or strained, causing miscommunication and conflicts.
RESULT: research loses credibility, agency loses credibility, research is late/deadlines likely missed.

Even if you plan to hire a professional MR agency to handle all aspects of the project's design and execution, it is best to be aware of these challenges. Even a great agency has limitations; by being educated about the MR process, you'll be in a better position to protect your company's investment.

FIRST THINGS FIRST: PLAN APPROPRIATELY

Although the task of hiring an MR agency to conduct custom research may sound pretty straightforward, to do it well takes some planning. How long will the whole process take? It really depends on the size of project. Figure 1.1 shows an example for a large-sized project—say $100,000 to $200,000. It also assumes that more than one person is involved in the process of defining the project and hiring an agency. In this example, the process starts with specifying the objectives and ends with agency selection—totaling six weeks.

So now that you have a rough idea of what the process looks like, let's get started with the first step; defining your market research goals (CHAPTER ONE).

Need some help with all of the jargon? See Appendix A for definitions of common Market Research terms.

FIGURE 1.1 AGENCY SELECTION SCHEDULE FOR A LARGE-SIZED PROJECT

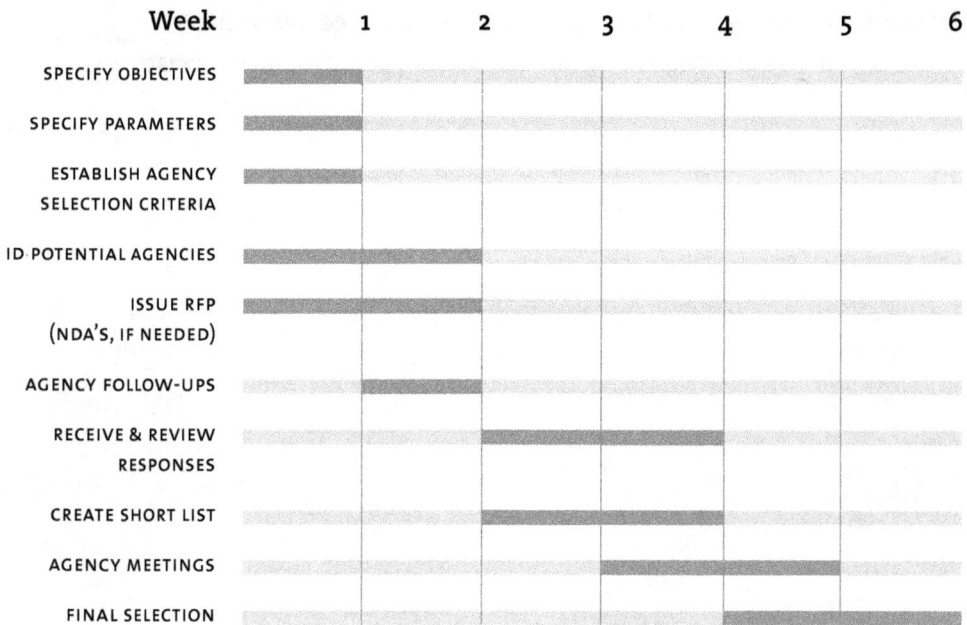

Week	1	2	3	4	5	6
SPECIFY OBJECTIVES	█					
SPECIFY PARAMETERS	█					
ESTABLISH AGENCY SELECTION CRITERIA	█					
ID POTENTIAL AGENCIES	█					
ISSUE RFP (NDA'S, IF NEEDED)	█					
AGENCY FOLLOW-UPS	█					
RECEIVE & REVIEW RESPONSES		█				
CREATE SHORT LIST		█				
AGENCY MEETINGS			█			
FINAL SELECTION				█		

Chapter One: Know Your Goals

HIGHLIGHTS

How to set MR project goals/ How to get buy-in from your internal team/ Sample goals

This sounds trite, but it is fundamental.

Once we have clarity about our MR goals, we are prepared to achieve four important things. First, we can decide if the goals are best met through in-house, syndicated, custom research, or other sources. Second, if needed, it informs the creation of a custom research request for proposal (RFP) that will actually result in useful proposals being submitted. Third, it informs our criteria for selecting a research agency. Fourth, it creates the criteria we will use to judge project success on completion. See the examples in Table 2.1.

TABLE 2.1 EXAMPLE BENEFITS OF KNOWING YOUR GOALS

My goal is...	It informs my RFP by...	It gives me agency selection critria such as...	It gives me success criteria, including...
...to learn with which target customer groups we need to invest more in basic brand awareness building.	Giving clear priority on project scope. The top priority is measuring brand awareness. We would like to test hypotheses about how it varies by geography and customer demo-graphics.	I need an agency that has a track record with brand awareness studies. Past experience in our industry is a plus.	On completion, we must have a prioritized list of customer groups among which we need to improve awareness.
...to select a logo from a set of four potential designs.	Giving clear priority on project scope. The top priority is getting feedback on four potential new logo treatments.	I need an agency that can handle a quantitative or a qualitative approach to logo testing.	On completion, we should have the four designs ranked in order, with pros and cons identified for each.

Do those examples seem too obvious? From this vantage point, they are. But once you are in the middle of planning a project—and are likely in the common scenario of having multiple goals—it gives you a framework for creating precise RFP content.

SETTING APPROPRIATE GOALS

When we're thinking about goals for MR projects, it's often helpful to think in terms of questions or hypotheses. Some examples of goals stated as questions follow:

- How can we improve sales of a product that hasn't met expectations?
- How can we improve our penetration within a specific customer group?
- Why have we experienced a sharp increase in customer defections?
- Which of three new product concepts should we invest in developing further?
- Which of several new possible geographic territories should we invest in for new distribution?
- What types of marketing messages are likely to resonate with our target customers as we roll out this new product or solution?
- What percentage of our target market knows we exist?
- What percentage of a specific customer group has favorable impressions of our brand? And how can we increase this percentage?

These are all examples of pretty specific questions that can serve as excellent goals to define a research project's scope. While your own questions may be different, use these as a guide for how to ask questions that are precise enough to be meaningful.

In some cases, you might actually already have hypotheses, and that's also a great way to define a project. Examples of hypotheses that a research project can be designed to test include the following:

- We have a hypothesis that awareness of our product is dramatically higher among 18- to 35-year-olds than among those 36 to 49.

- We have a hypothesis that we can charge a premium for product X if it includes feature Y.

- We have a hypothesis that packaging preferences for our category vary dramatically by world region.

- We have a hypothesis that our new product is likely to cannibalize sales of one of our other products.

- We have a hypothesis that customer buying criteria are shifting such that customers are now primarily buying on price.

- We have a hypothesis that sales of new product A are lackluster because our channel partners are not adequately trained with it.

Whether in the form of questions or hypotheses, specifying, agreeing on, and documenting specific goals at project onset is the first step. Whether you have questions or specific hypotheses, **once you identify your top two or three priorities, you can proceed to the next steps: choosing the best option for meeting your goals, writing the RFP, and identifying potential agencies.**

Wait a minute. "Just two or three?" you ask. Yes. The most successful custom MR projects have one or two high-level goals, three at the most. Of course, under that level, there can be several subgoals. For example, in a case where the primary goal is to measure brand awareness among a target customer group, appropriate subgoals might be (a) to understand how that varies by region or country, and (b) to test how it compares relative to competitive brands. So, yes, stick to just a few high-level goals—but of course, each may have a set of appropriate subgoals.

GO VS. NO GO. OR, ARE MY GOALS BEST MET THROUGH CUSTOM MR?

Once you identify the key goals, it is time to step back, take a good, hard look at them, and ask yourself this:

What is the best way to meet these goals? Is it, in fact, through custom MR? Or does the information, perhaps, already exist? Maybe it exists in an off-the-shelf research report, a syndicated service, or another source completely.

Many information sources exist and may be readily available with a little detective work. Here are some common places to check for existing information:

- Industry associations

- Company library/internal website

- Company consultants

- Internal market research department

- Other agencies (ad agency, PR agency)

- Trade magazines

Conducting MR In-house

Once you decide you do need primary market research, the next question becomes: can we do it ourselves, or should we hire an agency? Thanks to great online tools like SurveyMonkey and Zoomerang, DIY is certainly an option. DIY is best used when the following conditions are met:

- You feel comfortable that you can write a questionnaire such that it will capture information objectively (and this may very well be the case if you are tackling a narrow topic and you really only need to ask, for example, eight to ten questions)

- You have time to do the project management in-house

- You have the skills in-house to clean the collected data and analyze it

- You have resources in-house that can analyze and report the findings in a way that will be credible to your internal colleagues

- You have access to a truly, high quality sample source

- You don't need the research to be blind (you are willing to reveal your company as the sponsor)

GOALS DEFINE THE MR RFP'S SCOPE

Assuming that you do decide custom MR is the best path, how will having these goals be used to start designing an RFP? First, it allows you to state very precisely what you need from this research—what the exact scope of this project is. Always put project goals, clearly stated, on the first page of the RFP. Don't bury them on Page 5. Let the agencies bidding on your work know right away if (a) this is a project for which they are qualified, and (b) how complex the project will be.

In addition, clear thinking early on about your goals can help you to provide even more detail about your project's scope. Consider the following:

- Are you more likely to be writing an RFP that would be seeking qualitative research expertise (in-depth interviews, focus groups, etc.) or quantitative approaches (statistical analyses, questionnaire design)?

- Or, are you looking for the research firms to recommend an approach? You can either request an approach or ask for their advice; either way is fine. If you do want them to recommend an approach, be sure that is clear in the RFP.

GOALS = AGENCY SELECTION CRITERIA

Now that you know your goals, you can start identifying potential MR suppliers. Which research agencies have a proven track record with this specific type of project? Which agencies have written relevant articles or posted relevant blogs?

There are hundreds of research agencies that provide custom research services, but most have areas of specialty. Even those that present themselves as being able to do everything usually have some primary focus in reality. Knowing what you need from the project will help you identify a list of suitable agencies to which you can send your RFP.

GOALS = SUCCESS CRITERIA

With clearly stated goals in hand, you also are prepared to easily document the criteria you will use to judge project success. As with any kind of project management, that's a key step for gaining clarity and generating buy-in and interest. For example, if your goal is to measure brand awareness, a logical success criterion could be, "Upon project conclusion, we will have measures of brand awareness for each of our top 20 geographic markets."

If you define the criteria for success upfront, you get the added benefit of being able to share that with internal clients. Has everyone agreed on what the criteria for success will be? Once agreement is reached, this becomes an important reference at project conclusion. It avoids a common end-of-project problem: You have come to the end of the project and are presenting the results. Someone in the audience says, "This is interesting, but it isn't what I wanted from this study." Now you can say, "Actually, here are the criteria we all agreed to at the beginning, and here is how these results map to the criteria. Can you help me understand where you see a gap?"

Especially for larger, high-visibility projects, you will have a large group at the final presentation. There is often one outlier—someone who either enjoys being a critic, or who just wasn't paying attention earlier in the process and now speaks up. Be prepared.

VERY RISKY BUSINESS

One of the most common reasons MR projects fail is because there is no specific agenda. Perhaps it started with one, but then the goals were diluted as different decision-makers started to contribute to the instrument design. It is a painfully common scenario: You start with a very precise MR study topic. Perhaps it's a project to test potential messages for a new advertising campaign. However, once word gets out that you're planning to do a custom MR project, it seems everybody wants to add "just" two or three questions to the questionnaire: "As long as you're talking to our customers, can you please ask them about distribution channels?" or, "Can you please find out if they've seen this recent ad we ran?"

Before you know it, a very precise, focused questionnaire that can be done with excellence has now become a questionnaire with an illogical flow that doesn't make any sense to the people who are taking the survey. Now, instead of being a nice 10-minute questionnaire, it's a 30-minute monster. Even worse, the people screened for the primary objective may be unqualified to answer these tangential questions—so the resulting data end up weak—and now all of those unwelcome survey vampires are unhappy internal clients!

Alas, it is time to be the survey cop. **Someone has to define, protect, and uphold the agreed upon project priorities**. Does that mean you should just say no to these requests? Of course not. Sometimes the requestor can be shown that the answers to their questions already exist. In their excitement to add on to a new project, perhaps they have forgotten to look for existing information. A little guidance about where the answers may possibly exist could solve the conflict. And if truly no readily available answers exist, it may simply be time to scope a new project to address their specific needs. Once you select the agency for your primary study, you may find some economies of scale by having them bid on this new project as well.

Why Is This So Risky?

If you decide to add questions to your instrument that are not specifically aligned with your primary goals, you have to keep in mind three things: fit, flow, and length.

- **Fit**. Are the people you're going to recruit for the primary goals also the right people to answer these new questions? If not, you might need to revamp the original sampling plan, which can drive up costs and introduce delays.

- Most studies require very specific samples (the people who will be qualified to take your questionnaire or participate in your focus group). For example, let's say the primary goal of this project is to measure awareness of your brand. You are likely interested in measuring awareness only among people who actually buy your product category (you might not want to measure awareness of your frozen pizza brand among people who never buy frozen pizza). You're going after a very specific audience.

- If you want to add questions outside of the original scope, you have to decide if the same population can answer the additional questions. Perhaps, instead, they would be best answered by a differently qualified group. Maybe now you would have to change your recruiting parameters to include both people who already buy your product category and those who do not. In the pizza example, perhaps your company is now thinking about extending its brand into frozen hamburgers; so now you want to find out if your brand has permission to enter that category. It may be valid to test your brand's permissions among people who do and do not currently buy frozen pizza.

- Unless you have a large budget for extra sampling, it's probably not going to be a good idea. If a project requires dramatically different lines of questioning for two separately qualified groups, it is almost always best to simply conduct two separate studies.

- **Flow**. Another thing to consider before adding extra questions to an instrument is this: Do the extra questions in any way bias participants' responses to the rest of the questionnaire?

That is, are we going to be introducing a topic or a concept that might somehow change how people would respond to subsequent questions? It is important to be careful about this. Will new questions need to be sequenced in a way that is awkward to respondents to avoid biasing responses?

- Of course, you also want to avoid asking questions that are too cognitively difficult or intrusive—you don't want to cause dropouts over secondary objectives.

- **Length**. For surveys, shorter durations mean higher response and completion rates. Unnecessarily long or complicated questionnaires can drive up costs and drive down data quality—and do so very quickly.

QUESTIONNAIRE LENGTH

To optimize compliance and data quality, questionnaires should be designed to take between five and 15 minutes to complete for the average respondent. Yes, there are people who'll say, "Oh no, 30 or 40 minutes is fine." Well, if your company has customers who truly love you and the questionnaire is only going to those customers, maybe you can get away with a long survey. Passionate customers are often eager to give you feedback. They are happy to take the time to complete the survey and be thoughtful throughout its duration.

In most cases, though, you cannot assume you have so much time and attention. In reality, the following statements are true:

- Many questionnaire projects are blind. That is, you don't want to reveal who's sponsoring the survey.

- Most questionnaire projects are not of just your current customers— you may be surveying prospects, competitors' customers, or a broad mix.

- Even if you are exclusively surveying customers, few companies have such ecstatic customer bases that they can get 40 minutes of attention.

Because of these issues, we know that in the real world, average questionnaire completion time is important. Long, laborious questionnaires result in high dropout rates and low data quality. It's obvious why dropout rates increase, but why does data quality drop? Because after about 10 minutes, respondents become impatient, lose interest, or otherwise get distracted. They start to rush through and become less careful about question wording and answer options. The more they rush, the higher the chances they are not reporting their attitudes and behaviors as accurately as possible.

To help prevent this, it is best to set expectations about questionnaire length early. Let your internal clients or colleagues know you have a firm maximum duration. If they won't listen to the logic, make them accountable with money: If you hire an agency for a project that was specified as 20 minutes, and it becomes 30 minutes, you **will** incur notable fee increases. Are they willing to share in that?

MANAGING QUESTIONNAIRE REAL ESTATE

In MR, we sometimes talk about questionnaire real estate, or how much space with which you have to work. It's good context to keep in mind as you write your RFP. It's also a useful way to help your internal colleagues understand that space is limited.

Typically, you can assume that 80 percent of your instrument's real estate is going to be dedicated to your primary objective (this is true for questionnaires and discussions guides). For example, if your primary goal is product concept testing, you can assume the following will roughly apply:

- 80 percent of your content is going to focus on the primary objective.

- 10 percent is going to be related to profiling and screening. In the case of questionnaires, there will be critical questions at the beginning and at the end of the instrument. Those at the beginning will screen people to make sure they meet your qualifications for the survey, and those at the end will capture profiling information so you can perform different types of analyses that will make the research meaningful to you.

- 10 percent might be available for additional contextual questions or secondary objectives. If there is a secondary objective to the study, you need to be clear with the agency you hire so it can plan the real estate accordingly. This also allows the agency to submit a proposal with suggestions about how to address both objectives in a meaningful way without compromising either.

MANAGING QUESTIONNAIRE LENGTH

There are exercises that you can do in team meetings to make sure that everybody buys into and has clarity about project goals. One exercise I do with clients is a design-your-dream-chart exercise called Chartstorming™. The comprehensive version of this exercise is useful for larger groups and otherwise complex situations. But for many cases, the simplified version described here works just as well (SEE TABLE 1.2).

First, assemble a group of 3 to 10 participants and set up a whiteboard or flip chart. Then have each person brainstorm about what would happen at the end of the project if they could only get five charts. Ask them to sketch these out on paper. And, yes, only five. So they get to project themselves: "It is the end of the project. I've just spent $50,000. If I only got five charts from my investment, what would they be?"

We are not looking to predict what the outcome would be, but to design and label the charts. Here are some examples of what these charts could be:

- A bar chart showing awareness of our brand by customer group.

- A chart showing propensity to pay a premium for specific features we're considering.

- A chart showing how we compare to our competitors in terms of perceived product reliability.

- A chart showing the importance of different product attributes to our male vs. female customers.

- A perceptual map that plots our product models along the axes of "perceived reliability" and "ease of use."

Next, nominate a facilitator to manage steps 2 and 3 as described in Table 1.2.

Obviously, many possibilities exist. Getting the team together to generate the priorities is a great way to get buy-in. It's a useful way to get people to think very clearly and precisely about what they truly need at the end of this research project.

If you go through this process and you find that a miracle happened and everyone agrees on those five charts, that's great! Perhaps we just designed an eight-minute survey. In reality, you likely will complete the exercise with five top picks and several secondary picks. That's fine—at least it's prioritized.

Another outcome is possible: sometimes at the end of this exercise, the group has defined 2 separate projects. That is a legitimate outcome. At least now we have precisely defined the needs, even if they can not be reasonably addressed in a single effort.

TABLE 1.2 CHARTSTORMING™ TEAM EXERCISE

Step 1	Get 3 to 10 people to join in and sketch five charts each.
Step 2	As a group, eliminate redundant charts, and then rate each remaining chart in terms of actionability and importance using a scale from 1 to 5. For example, if Chart 12 is rated a 3 on actionability and a 4 on importance, its total is 7.
Step 3	Rank order the charts using this approach, then identify and review the top five. Discuss areas of agreement and disagreement. Agree upon next steps.

HIGHLIGHTS

Common Market Research project types defined/ Conducting blind research/ B2B versus B2C considerations

As you start to plan your RFP, it's a good idea to think about the "type" of project you will be doing. By now, you should have your goals—again, stated as either questions or hypotheses. But you want to make it crystal clear to your RFP recipients what this project is about, and framing it in their vernacular will help you do this. Common project types include the following:

- Product concept testing

- Market segmentation

- Message testing

- Customer loyalty/customer satisfaction

- Win-loss research

- Brand awareness tracking

- Needs discovery

There are more, but we'll use these common types.

PRODUCT CONCEPT TESTING

There are many different flavors of product concept testing, but two types are most common. The first type is about identifying which of several concepts are worth pursuing, and the second is about taking a concept you've already chosen to develop and determining how to optimize its features for maximum market penetration.

In the first case, you haven't actually decided what product you're going to develop. Perhaps you have three or four different potential ideas and you're trying to figure out which are worth pursuing further, perhaps to the point of developing a prototype. This is a great stage at which to use MR. The outcomes from this type of study typically include a prioritized set of concepts, and usually include one or more of the following:

- Perceived pros and cons of each concept.

- Perceived attribute or feature must-haves vs. nice-to-haves.

- Perceived value proposition of each concept (how a customer would justify or rationalize its purchase). In B2B studies, this might include an expected return on investment (ROI) model.

- Indications of each concept's differentiation compared to competitors or substitutes.

In the other common type of product concept testing, you've already decided what the product is going to be and you are trying to optimize it. Typically, these projects are designed to do one or more of the following:

- Prioritize which features are going to be most important to potential buyers.

  - This informs decisions about which features to emphasize on packaging, in ads, and so on. This is often referred to as messaging.

- Determine what else could be bundled with the product to maximize adoption.

  - For example, if your company is about to manufacture a new children's toy, you might do research to understand which types of accessories should be bundled with the toy to command the highest share of preference or the greatest price premium.

- Determine which features have to be in a first-release version vs. subsequent releases.

  - This is usually done for software products, for which there might be a sense of urgency to get the product to market quickly—even if that means doing so without all of the features available.

- Test aesthetic or user interface appeal.

  - For example, perhaps you are designing home theater equipment, and you know that it's important that the choice of colors, shape, and controls (dials, buttons, LEDs) appeals to your target market.

MARKET SEGMENTATION

The premise of market segmentation is that to maximize sales to a large population of customers, it is best to divide it into logical subgroups. The assumption is that by dividing one large, amorphous mass into subgroups, you can fine-tune your product, messaging, support, or distribution channels to meet the specific needs of unique customer groups. Thus, the goal is to use a market segmentation model to improve marketing success and optimize marketing ROI.

Segmentation models vary from basic to complex, and the approaches to developing and applying them is a topic for an entire book itself. But here are some examples:

- EXAMPLE 1: A telecommunications company selling mobile phone services might segment its market based on complexity of needs. One customer group might only need voice service, and very little volume at that. Another group might primarily use mobile texting services. Yet another might be a heavy user of mobile phones for voice, text, email, and web browsing. By identifying distinct patterns in customer needs, the company can optimize product bundles and target them at the correct audiences.

- EXAMPLE 2: A hotel chain that caters to families might simply segment its market based on income level and travel frequency. The chain might find that a group of moderate income-frequent travelers exists that is swayed by certain loyalty program rewards. It might find another important group exists—that is more swayed by on-site amenities. With this information, the hotel can optimize its offerings and loyalty programs to appeal to each group's unique needs.

Market segmentation studies are fairly involved. They are often multi-phased projects that can get very complex, especially for global organizations. In fact, in my experience, market segmentation studies are among the most complex types of projects and have a higher risk of failure as compared to other studies. Even when completed as planned, many clients find it challenging to truly apply the results.

Market segmentation can be done with both consumer and business populations. That said, the studies for B2B populations are very different than those for B2C populations. Take this into consideration when selecting potential agencies for this type of project. A firm that has strong experience in consumer segmentation does not necessarily have B2B segmentation expertise.

MESSAGE TESTING

The goal of message testing studies is to find out which messages are most likely to resonate with the target market and which are perceived as credible from the company issuing the messages. The premise is that most organizations could use multiple messages, but finding the best ones are important to marketing success.

Message testing is often conducted using qualitative research techniques—athough exceptions certainly exist—because you usually want to view body language reactions and hear people talk in their own words about the messages being tested.

In addition, a common exercise in this type of study is to discover what brands people think would use a given message. Let's say one message you want to test is labeled Message A. Research participants are asked to name what companies they think would use Message A. They are also asked from which companies they think Message A is most believable. After all, you will waste a lot of money if you choose a marketing message that positions you as something that nobody's going to believe. CVS would probably not be successful positioning itself as a retailer of luxury goods because nobody has experienced the brand in that way.

These studies also can be designed to answer the following types of questions:

- Which message will differentiate us the most from our competitors?

- Which message will be perceived as consistent with our overall positioning strategy?

- Which message will seem most in-tune with customers' needs?

CUSTOMER LOYALTY

Customer loyalty studies are often considered a key strategic type of research that should be done on an annual—if not quarterly—basis. Many large companies closely track customer loyalty to catch potential issues before they spread. Companies with smaller customer bases usually do these studies once a year.

In the past, we usually referred to customer satisfaction studies, but the vernacular these days more often centers on loyalty. The MR field learned over the years that satisfied customers aren't necessarily loyal customers. Because the point of research is to find out how we can encourage desirable behaviors (like additional purchases, subscription renewals, or upsell opportunities), we want to uncover how to build and maintain loyalty. We want to know how to keep customers loyal so they will be unlikely to defect to a competing brand.

Customer loyalty studies can be designed to answer different types of questions, such as these:

- How does repeat purchase behavior for your brand vary by income level, gender, or household type?

- Among businesses, how do repeat purchase behaviors for your brand vary by company size, vertical industry, decision-making level, and years of experience?

- What types of customer service experiences are associated with increased loyalty?

- Does satisfaction with specific aspects of your product predict loyal behaviors?

- Does length of relationship predict loyalty? At what phases in the relationship are you at greatest risk for losing loyalty?

One last note about these studies: Many research firms conduct customer loyalty and satisfaction research, but there are also several firms that specialize in it. These firms have focused entire practices on such studies, and some have developed their own methodologies and frameworks for indentifying the factors that best predict satisfaction and loyalty measures.

WIN-LOSS RESEARCH

Win-loss research is another common category of MR study. It typically applies more to B2B research than to consumer research, though exceptions do exist.

Whether B2B or B2C, win-loss studies are typically designed to answer four questions:

1. What factors most commonly lead to a sales win?

2. What factors most commonly lead to a sales loss?

3. How frequently do these factors occur?

4. What steps can be taken to mitigate loss factors?

This is a kind of study that could be treated qualitatively or quantitatively, depending on how many sales you have: Is it enough that quantitative research is even feasible?

This type of study also has a unique aspect, in that it typically requires that you share with your agency the lists of customers who have either purchased from or chosen not to purchase from your company. The agency will want to talk to a good number of those who have selected your company as well as those who selected your competitors, so that it can understand what's really driving wins vs. losses.

As an example, one such study that I did was for a client in the telecommunications industry. While this client had a lot of great information from its sales department on what the factors were, it needed an objective measure of how often each one was actually occurring. For example, it knew that it was more likely to win when a prospect valued one-stop-shopping. But it didn't know how often this was leading to a win. Ten percent of the time? Or fifty? And if it was, in fact, a significant win driver, how could the client do a better job of using this to its advantage?

BRAND AWARENESS

Both consumer and B2B companies track brand awareness and perceptions to inform decisions such as the following:

- How much to invest in brand-building activities.

- What mix of media or channels to invest in (what ratio of print, television, radio, Internet, etc.).

- Which ad campaigns to continue or retire.

- How to adjust brand-building investments by geography.

- How to deploy sales resources to build or leverage brand awareness.

Typically, brand awareness research is not something you do just once. You usually do it as a tracker (quarterly or annually), or as a before-and-after study. For example, if you are about to launch a major new ad campaign, you might measure brand awareness before and after it runs to gauge its impact. If the impact was positive, you have some feedback on what works. If the impact was not so great, you hope you can catch the problem early enough to make corrections.

As an example, one brand awareness tracking study I did was for a PC manufacturer. We did a quarterly data collection to continuously keep up with what was happening. This client advertised using various channels, so it needed to know what was and wasn't working to help maximize advertising ROI.

In these studies, you measure more than brand awareness. Usually, you're also measuring key brand perceptions. This involves gathering unaided and aided perceptions of your brand (whether a company-level or product-level brand). Often, perceptions of key competitors are also gathered so that you know how awareness and perceptions of your brand compare. Why is that useful? Let's say you learn that 60 percent of your target market perceives your brand as socially responsible. You might think that's not bad. But what if 95 percent of them think your three biggest competitors are? In that context, that 60 percent figure doesn't look so great. Competitive data give you a more actionable perspective.

NEEDS DISCOVERY

MR agencies are often engaged to discover the unmet needs of the client's target market, whether it's a market that is already being served or one the client plans on serving. For example, let's say your business primarily serves high-income households with consumer electronics products. You might want to do periodic surveys to answer questions like these:

- How does that market select consumer electronics products?

- What other consumer electronics products do they buy? Which are they happy with?

- What are they not happy with, or, what are their current frustrations that could potentially be met with new products, solutions, or services?

Unfortunately, this type of study is not as common as others. All too often, companies create a product or a solution and then work very hard to find a way to sell it (the, "If we build it, they will come," mentality). **Obviously, in an ideal world, a company would first do discovery to understand what the market really wants and needs, and then come up with products and**

solutions accordingly. When companies do this type of research, it can deliver a significant competitive advantage; it's pretty likely your competitors have not invested in that type of research.

SPECIAL STUDIES

Of course, in certain industries there are specialty studies as well. Here are some examples:

- In the technology sector, there are specialty studies on technology adoption plans. These are often B2B projects, where surveys of IT decision-makers (CIOs, vice presidents of IT, IT directors) seek to find out what technologies they plan to adopt, which they've actually budgeted for, which they plan to evaluate, and so forth.

- In the pharmaceutical industry, doctors are surveyed to gauge their propensity to prescribe specific types of pharmaceuticals.

- For website testing, eyeball tracking studies literally track how users' eyes scan the screen.

REVEALING SPONSORSHIP—OR NOT

Now that you are familiar with common types of MR studies, you'll be better able to communicate your needs and expectations to potential agencies.

After you ponder project scope (i.e., what type of MR study you want to fund), another important consideration is whether or not the research will be blind. In the world of research, blind means that the sponsor is kept anonymous. You probably have experienced this yourself. Perhaps you have received a call at home asking you to participate in a survey from XYZ research company. XYZ doesn't tell you who is sponsoring the survey, so this research is blind.

Once the researcher starts asking questions, you might have an educated guess as to the sponsoring company. For example, if the researcher asks you questions about automobiles and keeps coming back to comparisons of Honda and Toyota, you might guess that one of those companies is the sponsor. Because you aren't sure, though, the assumption is that your answers will be as unbiased as possible. In contrast, if you knew the survey was sponsored by Toyota, and you happen to be a loyal Toyota customer, you might give biased results—unintentional, perhaps, but still biased.

In most cases the ideal is to keep research blind, to minimize the risk of bias. However, two common exceptions do exist.

- EXCEPTION 1: The project is being done using your own customer lists. In this case, due to privacy concerns, you may need to reveal yourself as the sponsor. Customers can get very upset if they feel their contact information has been shared with third parties without their express permission. In some cases, there can even be legal ramifications. For example, perhaps you want to do a customer satisfaction study among recent purchasers; this will clearly not be blind—they will know you are the sponsor. If you are not sure what is required, ask your legal department.

- EXCEPTION 2: You are surveying a very hard-to-find population, and you have to take every possible step to get qualified participants. For example, you are looking to survey people who use a very niche software product—not many people use it—and when you are able to reach these precious few, you need to maximize the chance they will comply with the request to take the survey. Sometimes revealing the sponsor can help get them interested. In this case, it's not ideal, but it might be an acceptable compromise.

SO I KNOW MY SCOPE AND IF I WANT IT BLIND. NOW WHAT?

Deciding what type of project you want to do and knowing whether or not you want it to be blind is critical information for your RFP. Stating this information precisely in your RFP tells bidders that you have put serious thought into your needs and that you're a reasonably educated customer.

POPULATION PARAMETERS: B2B AND B2C

In framing the scope of your project, think about the respondents who will
be able to give you actionable data. Are you researching attitudes and behaviors of consumers? Businesses? Perhaps both? This has important implications for agency selection, sample source options, and questionnaire design.

AGENCY SELECTION

Some research firms are far more comfortable with consumer research than
with B2B research. Don't assume all research firms can cover both. There are
specific challenges in both B2B and B2C research, and you want a firm that
has the appropriate experience. Check out the client names a firm lists on
its website: Are they heavily weighted toward retail companies? Business
services companies? Consumer goods manufacturers? Technology companies? Are they truly diverse?

If you are seeking B2B expertise, be especially vigilant about assessing a
potential supplier's relevant qualifications. **B2B studies are notoriously difficult because it is much harder to get business professionals to agree to
participate in research.** They are often too busy or might even be prohibited
by company policy (due to confidentiality concerns). The more senior a business participant you want, the harder (and riskier) it gets.

SAMPLE SOURCE OPTIONS

Your agency will provide recommendations about how to find qualified
research participants (the sample), but you should still be educated about
this in the interest of project quality. Here are four important facts for you
to know:

1. Sample sources for both B2B and B2C projects vary, and so do their quality.
   Be sure to ask what the agency will do to assess the quality of respondents.

   - If your agency says it uses research panels, be aware: Panels are
     not by definition high-quality sources. We all wish they were, but it
     just isn't the case. Some panels have more quality assurance steps

to validate respondent identity than others, and other panels are notoriously over-surveyed.

2. Ask what the sample source is, and how many sources the agency intends to use. A professional agency will be able to give you a clear, credible response. If you get a vague, confusing response, beware.

3. If you need to cover both consumer and business populations, be sure you will have a way of knowing which respondents came from which sample source. At some point, you likely will want to look at their answers separately, and compare and contrast them.

4. You can supply the sample, but only do so if:

- **It's a clean list.** If you provide a database that is out of date (more than 5 percent of the records have "bad" phone, email, and other critical fields), you will delay the project and incur extra costs.

- **You have permission.** You might possess a list that you'd like to use, but do you have permission to do so? Do you have permission to share the list with outside suppliers? If you are doing international research, do different laws apply to list members in a given country? If you are at all unsure, check with your legal department. You might have to disclose your sponsorship (so the research will not be blind, as described earlier), or you might have other boundaries.

- **It won't bias the research or restrict the analysis.** For example, is this a list of people you know are likely to be favorable to your brand—and is this a study on brand perceptions? Obviously, that would skew the results. That example is obvious, but others are more subtle. The suitability of your in-house list is something your agency can advise you on, given your specific needs.

- **(For B2B studies) If you have the right contact names.** For example, you may have a great list of companies with purchasing department contacts listed. But if the survey requires reaching people who are, for example, in the Human Resources department, that isn't going to help.

B2B AND B2C CONSIDERATIONS FOR QUESTIONNAIRE DESIGN

How we ask questions of business customers versus consumer customers can vary dramatically. For example, consider research conducted on behalf of PC manufacturers. You can seek the same information from both audiences, but the way that you approach them needs to be adjusted. Consumers are generally less familiar with technical specifications than their business counterparts, so you need to modify the wording to make a questionnaire accessible for them. Turning them off with "geek speak" won't help get the information you need.

An agency familiar with your target audiences will know how to modify and present questions so that they are appropriate, but it's always a good idea to sanity check this yourself. If your study is consumer-focused, look over the questionnaire yourself. Could you, as a consumer, understand the questions and the answer options? Could your spouse? Your parent? Your neighbor? A few minutes spent checking the questionnaire content will save you a lot of pain down the road. You may even request to have access to pre-test interviews to approve the process before full fielding begins. While this does add time, this step has saved many a career! You don't want to present the final results and have an executive point out, "If I had seen this question I wouldn't have understood how to answer it . . . so I don't think we can trust the responses." Ouch.

Chapter Three: Considering the Internal Audience

Uncovering your audience's needs/ Designing a project your colleagues will embrace/ Research readiness

Is your organization ready for custom MR? Will the people, your internal audience, actually use it?

I work with a lot of different organizations and have found a wide spectrum of "readiness" for MR. Some firms have been very sophisticated users of primary MR, and thus their internal audiences are used to seeing it, reading it, and digesting it. At the other extreme, I've worked with plenty of companies that were new to primary MR, so their internal audiences weren't equipped or comfortable with the process or the results.

A Common Scenario

One very common scenario is that a company that has traditionally relied heavily on secondary research and analyst reports now faces some key business challenges. Those old sources aren't delivering the needed insights, so they turn to primary research. Great! But, if they are not well-prepared, they enter into the process with unrealistic expectations about what can be achieved or false assumptions about cost and time requirements. The chances for failure are high in these cases.

If you feel your audience is not quite ready, it's best to do some training as a preemptive strike. The training need not be elaborate. It can be as simple as a brief workshop to present the lifecycle of an MR project (showing the various stages, typical milestones, etc.), or it could be written documentation about how to interpret MR data. If you feel some such training is in order, ask your research supplier—they may very well have such materials readily available.

Objectively assessing your internal audience's readiness for MR is important for a few reasons, including the following:

- Your internal audience's sophistication with MR has implications for the type of research you do.

- It has implications for how you will want to deliver the results at the end of a project.

- It will inform your choices about how to prepare your audience for the delivery of final results.

Where do we start? By evaluating our audience on four parameters, shown in Table 3.1.

TABLE 3.1 MEASURING AUDIENCE READINESS FOR MR

Item	Key questions
Receptivity	Is your audience open-minded about MR? Do you have a lot of research skeptics?
Data type preferences	In your organization, is there a general preference for "hard numbers" (quantitative research) or for stories (qualitative)? Does one type of information influence key decision-makers more than the other?
Sophistication	Do they know how to read charts and graphs? Do they know what a cross-tab is? Do they understand the limitations of research, or are they likely to have unrealistic expectations?
Attention span	How much of their own time will they give to the project, either during the planning phase (when their input might be needed) or at the conclusion (when they need to receive and read the results)?

If you feel you need more guidance in reflecting on these items, see the self-assessment quiz at the end of this chapter.

RESEARCH RECEPTIVITY

Will your internal audience be receptive to research results? How can you maximize receptivity? Careful thought about this will help you create an RFP and agency selection criteria that ultimately will affect your project's success. Here are some points to ponder:

- Is your company full of skeptics who will reject any results that conflict with their personal opinions or preconceived beliefs?

- Is your organization full of people who will only accept good news and will shoot the messenger if there's bad news?

- Do you have people who are going to be cynical about the results no matter what—whether it's qualitative or quantitative, even if the results are based on large numbers of participants?

- If your research will be among your current customer base, will your salespeople object to "their" customers' information being shared?

A little bit of cynicism is fine. In fact, it's healthy. I like it when people ask tough questions because it shows me that they're paying attention. And let's be honest: There is some shabby research out there, people should ask questions.

Still, excessive cynicism is counterproductive. To keep it from derailing the research process, it's a good idea to assess it and determine its root causes. Be sure to understand why they are inclined to be cynics:

- Did a past research project go terribly awry? You need to find out what happened, so that preemptive steps can be taken to avoid a repeat. If relevant, those steps can be stated as project requirements in the RFP.

  - For example, did a past project fail because the agency did not keep you informed of deviations from quota requirements? Then the RFP should state clearly that you will require quota updates daily during the data collection process.

- Does your audience have unanswered questions about the agency's qualifications? If so, it's usually an easy fix. If you know certain credentials are required to make an agency acceptable, ask for them in the RFP.

  - Are only firms with lots of PhDs on staff good enough? Fine. Get them. Do you have colleagues who prefer agencies that have notable experience conducting research in China? Great—ask agencies to give examples of their data collection experience in China.

- Are they skeptical about finding qualified respondents? This is a common, legitimate concern. An agency should be able to give you reasonable and precise information about their sample sources and the techniques used to qualify respondents and data check responses.

In many cases, a little forethought and preparation of a preemptive strike can go a long way toward overcoming cynicism. In contrast, avoiding the issue only leads to heartache.

DATA TYPE PREFERENCES

What types of information will your audience find most useful? Easiest to understand? Most suitable for taking action? Market research can deliver information in various forms—and it isn't always obvious which one is best (see Table 3.2).

TABLE 3.2 COMMON DATA TYPE CHOICES

Information Types	Examples
Quantitative: Hard numbers	A survey of 1,000 customers, delivered in tables, cross-tabs, charts, and graphs. The results are statistically testable.
Quantitative: Soft numbers	A survey of 100 customers, perhaps more directional than statistical. In some cases, from known, highly qualified respondents (such as a customer list). These numbers tell a story, but aren't necessarily statistically representative.
Qualitative: Text format	Select quotes from focus groups or research interviews.
Qualitative: Video format	Select video clips from focus groups or research interviews.
Qualitative: Observational	Ethnography (e.g., videotapes of shoppers as they examine a shelf display).

As you look through Table 3.2, ask yourself if your group is more swayed by certain types of information than others. Company cultures vary in terms of the types of information that have real influence. Is this an audience that's strongly influenced by hard numbers? Is this an audience that's more influenced by stories and anecdotes? Do they need to see it to believe it? Do they need sheer volume of data to be convinced of any finding? Are they turned on by elegant analyses? Do they tune-out as soon as they see a bar chart?

PREFERENCES FOR QUALITATIVE

In some companies—even very large ones—qualitative research is more influential than quantitative. Some executive-level decision-makers are far more comfortable with stories and verbatim quotes than with numbers. That might be surprising. You would expect the management team of, say, a leading consumer goods manufacturer, to embrace hard numbers. But when it comes to making decisions about topics such as product development, marketing strategies, or customer satisfaction tactics, in some cases, stories resonate the most.

Also, in reality, it's easy to try to discredit quantitative information. Even if you've done a survey of 2,000 customers and you found out your customer satisfaction scores aren't what they could be, there are going to be executives who will find ways to knock holes in that. Even if their criticisms aren't valid, it can really dilute the impact of the research as it gets rolled out through the organization. If you know your audience includes likely naysayers who will nitpick your numbers, it can make sense to do a study with qualitative methods. Of course, it is not always an either-or choice: If budget permits, a combination can be ideal.

In one case, I was doing a win-loss study. As described earlier, win-loss is a topic that can be done either qualitatively or quantitatively. But this client had thousands of accounts that would need to be represented to understand what was really driving wins vs. losses. As a researcher seeking to match objectives to methodology, I would have preferred a quantitative measure so that at the end of the project I could have made statements like, "The top reasons that you lose sales are X, Y, and Z, and that applies to 20, 30, and 40 percent of losses, respectively."

However, during the sales process, it became apparent that this audience would not be receptive to hard numbers. No matter what the numbers were, somebody would refute them. It would be much more credible to come out with stories. So instead of a quantitative approach, we used qualitative techniques (in the form of 20-minute, in-depth interviews). In the end, the final report was full of customer quotes about brand choices—there were very few charts.

As an aside, the client ended up spending nearly 30 percent more on the research study than it would have using a quantitative methodology. So was it economically efficient? No. But was it audience-appropriate? Yes.

PREFERENCES FOR QUANTITATIVE

In other organizations, the strong preference is for quantitative data—hard numbers, based on large sample sizes. This is especially common in engineering-driven companies and financial institutions—where the management teams often seem more comfortable with numbers than with anecdotes.

In these situations, qualitative research can be the easily dismissed methodology. And I have seen clients who wanted to do quantitative research even when a qualitative methodology would better meet the objectives. After all, qualitative methods also can be refuted. Common challenges from qualitative research cynics include:

- What if you only talked to outliers? This information could be misleading!

- I think the research participants were just being polite to the focus group moderator—I don't think they gave really candid information.

The bottom line: **If there is a conflict between the best methodology for the project's objectives and the best for internal audience needs, it is necessary to weight your choice heavily toward the audience.** The research will be useless if it doesn't have an impact on actual decision-making.

SOPHISTICATION

Is your audience comfortable reading data? Would they read a large set of charts and graphs and understand them? Have they seen questionnaires in the past, such that they understand that there is a bit of science and art to the design? Do they embrace elegant data models?

Those of us in research often forget that not everyone is comfortable reading charts and numbers. Even if you label charts carefully (always a good idea in any case), not everyone "gets" them. Some people get tripped up reading the most basic statistics.

If your audience is unsophisticated in terms of data analysis, you will want something in your RFP asking about training options or creative ideas for presenting results to your audience. If you ask your research agency, they should be able to give you some options.

ATTENTION SPAN

How much of your audience's attention can you realistically get? Even if they are receptive, how much of an effort are they likely to make to digest and apply the research? How much hand-holding will they need? **Once a final report is delivered, can you trust that they will take the initiative to read it, come back with questions, and actually apply the results?**

One step to take is to set expectations: Let internal clients know early on how much time they will need to invest for the project to be a success. Let them know at what critical junctures their involvement is necessary. Let them know they should reserve time to receive and read the final results.

It would be a lot easier if the sucess of a market research project was judged at the point of report delivery or final presentation. But the brutal reality is that your audience will judge the project's success based on the extent to which they use it.

That's right. A market research project manager can spend three months planning, executing, and delivering a great project. But if the internal audience is unprepared to understand it, too busy to read it, or finds the results too cumbersome to navigate, the project will be perceived as a failure. It's up to us to make sure the audience is ready, willing, and able.

DEALING WITH HARD-CORE SKEPTICS

Do you anticipate a lot of pushback no matter what the final project results are? Maybe you are expecting the study will deliver some "bad news"? If so, there are a few things that can minimize resistance to research results.

1. **Get audience input early.** The first step is including people early in the research design process. I'm not saying that you want a committee of 30 people participating in questionnaire draft reviews; that's crazy and can only lead to disaster. Still, at the kickoff meeting, make sure you've got people from all the relevant lines of business, divisions, or departments who can participate in generating hypotheses or key questions that will drive the instrument design process. If you include these people early in the process, there's a lot less risk they're going to challenge the results at the end. After all, now they've got some vested interest in it. If you listen to their input, you can incorporate at least some of it, and your research report should reflect this.

2. **Address likely criticisms before they do.** Another way to head off end-of-project cynicism is to be very careful about how you describe the sample population to your audience. One of the greatest areas of cynicism at the end of a project occurs when somebody doesn't like the results and immediately concludes, "You must have talked to the wrong people. You obviously didn't talk to actual customers. You clearly talked to people who weren't qualified."

Hopefully, that wasn't the case and you can be certain the respondents were, indeed, qualified. Still, questioning respondent quality is a very easy way to derail research results. That's why this is an important item to ask potential agencies about; you want an agency that has a strong sampling plan, so that when you get asked, you have ample proof points (recall page 32). Then, you really just need a preemptive strike early in the presentation to communicate all of this clearly. It's usually one of the first slides in my presentations: a statement about sample sources and the qualification criteria used.

3. **Remind the audience about cognitive dissonance, or that they can't have it both ways.**

I also like to use humor as a preemptive strike. At the beginning of a final results presentation, I often say, "Today you are going to hear a lot of things. You are going to hear about attitudes and behaviors as reported by your prospects or customers. Some results will be consistent with your own experiences with customers and prospects, and the results will basically confirm what you already suspect. However, you might also hear some things that are new, and (with a little bit of humor) you cannot pick and choose. You cannot look at a research project and decide that you believe the things that you want to believe, but anything that you don't like is obviously false. It doesn't work that way. Either you buy into the research, or you don't buy into the research."

Another good idea for somebody presenting MR results is to remember that ultimately you are only the messenger. You've created a research project that gathers and presents the attitudes and behaviors of customers and prospects. Simply point out that you are presenting what customers and prospects have reported.

4. **For vocal, hard-core cynics, offer them options for validating the research.**
If they have an issue with the research results, there are easy ways to gauge whether or not the research results are, in fact, valid. Here are two common approaches:

- TRIANGULATION. You can triangulate it against other research results. Seek out other related studies, census data, analyst reports, and so on, and look for data points that might show supporting context. It's a best practice in any case, and one that is often overlooked.

- COLLECT MORE DATA. You can select a handful of research partici-pants, assuming you have the rights to do this, and conduct follow-up interviews. This can be used to confirm their validity and give you additional insight into their responses. You also can opt to col-lect another 100 or 200 responses, and see whether or not you continue to get consistent results. Your internal colleagues might have to spend a bit more money, but if they're saying that the research isn't valid, this option can be offered.

If you offer some options, even your hard-core skeptics should be satisfied.

5. **Pre-brief likely hard-core cynics.** Give these people a one-on-one sneak peek, and this way you can hear and respond to their issues before the big presentation. They will be less likely to disrupt the presentation if they feel their concerns have been addressed.

Self-Quiz: How Ready is Your Audience for Custom Market Research?

Answer the questions below as objectively as possible. With a little reflection, you will find that your answers reveal guidance for both A) preparing your audience for the research process, and B) designing a project that will meet their needs.

- How often are primary MR results presented to this audience? Less than once a year? Less than once every three years?

- What influences your key stakeholders more: detail-rich stories about customers, or hard numbers?

- Are key internal clients likely to actually read the research? Or will they want key take-aways only?

- Are there senior-level people in your company who are MR advocates? Whose endorsement can bring a sense of credibility to the process?

- What is the attitude when discussions of MR come up? Do executives tend to shy away because they think it is a waste of money? Or are they eager to learn more about customer attitudes and behaviors?

- If the research delivers an unexpected finding, how would the executives respond? Would they consider the result? Dismiss it immediately? Ask for backup? Be polite about it but not take action?

- Is your audience more accustomed to syndicated research than custom MR? Do they understand the respective strengths and weaknesses of each?

- Will key stakeholders be willing to invest some time upfront? That is, will they be willing to participate in a kickoff meeting? To participate in milestone meetings?

- Will key internal clients take the time to attend an in-person presentation at project conclusion? Will they need one-on-one debriefs?

- Will they know how to apply the results? Will they need some post-project support to help make this happen?

Chapter Four: Leveraging Existing Research

HIGHLIGHTS
*Using existing research to minimize risks/ Where to find existing research
(internal and external sources)*

Before funding a new MR study, it is always wise to make sure you understand what relevant research already exists. Here are five reasons why:

1. **The answers to your current questions might already exist.** Perhaps with a little digging, you will find that the research already has been conducted within the company, but not shared very effectively. You might be surprised how often this happens. The last thing you want is to proceed with the research, complete it, pay the bills for it, and then find out at the final results presentation that previous research had been conducted. Everyone involved loses credibility when this happens— and it does happen.

I have seen this happen in really ugly ways. Once I was doing a project for a large software company. At the final presentation, their MR manager and I presented some important findings, some of which we knew would be controversial. Imagine our dismay when an executive challenged some of these conclusions by citing similar research the company had done the year before! The MR manager and I had no knowledge of this research. As it turned out, the previous research had been based on a population with very different screening criteria, so we were later able to understand why the two studies had different results. But it was too late: the presentation's momentum was completely destroyed. The lesson is this: You need to know about any other relevant research, if for no other reason than if it does refute your conclusions, (a) you will be able to explain why, and (b) if conflicts truly exist, you can offer a course of action to uncover why.

2. **A research agency might already have a relationship with your firm,** and might have an internal track record of performing well. Your company, even if a different division or business unit, might have a relationship that can be leveraged. A research agency that performed well in the past will have good contextual knowledge. An agency that already has insights into your markets, customer behaviors, product lines, and company culture, has an advantage over those that do not. As an added benefit, if your executives already perceive the agency as credible (or as a trusted partner), your project will gain an instant credibility halo that would be lacking if you use a new, unknown agency (which must prove itself to be a reliable source).

3. **Important contextual data might be available** that will help with the research's design and execution. Perhaps in your research excavation, you dig up projects that don't address the current questions but do provide important context. The following is a real-world example of how this helps you ensure project success:

> Let's say you are planning a study of people who currently buy frozen entrees. After some research, you find a past study that showed attitudes and behaviors among this population vary notably by the number of entrees they buy per month (less than five, six to 10, or more than 10). Great! Now you know that in your current study, you need to consider including a quota that will distribute your sample along this parameter. Imagine if you had completed the study without knowing this. You might have—by sheer misfortune—ended up with a sample that was primarily people who buy fewer than five entrees per month. Or you might not have known to capture this variable at all, and you wouldn't have been able to get a cross-tab on it at the end of the project.

What is a Cross-tab?

A cross-tab is a simple table that shows how answers to a question vary by different respondent subgroups. As the simple example in Table 4.1 shows, a cross-tab table is a great way to compare responses very quickly. In this case, one can readily see that females are less likely to have a very high level of satisfaction with Company A's Customer Service, as compared to males.

TABLE 4.1 CROSS-TAB EXAMPLE

Satisfaction with Company A's customer service	Total responses (400)	Males (200)	Females (200)
Very high	230 (57.5%)	130 (65%)	100 (50%)
Neutral	120 (30%)	50 (25%)	70 (35%)
Very low	50 (12.5%)	20 (10%)	30 (15%)

4. **Establishing triangulation points.** Is research available to you on the same or even a related topic? If so, it could provide important triangulation points.

Triangulation points are data that can help you to do the following:

- Quantify a relevant customer behavior.

- Confirm existence of a related customer attitude.

- Size a potential demographic group.

- Reality-check a result using a different data source (such as scanner data).

5. **To identify potential risks.** You might find that similar, past studies done by your company had encountered obstacles. What were they? Is the current study likely to encounter the same obstacles? If you are forewarned, can you become forearmed? How can you mitigate these risks?

> Let me give you an example of what I mean. I once worked with a client who had done some research in the past, and had a really hard time getting realistic data from its target market about actual purchase plans. This was a company that sold a specific category of IT equipment. Whenever it went out and asked people about their plans to purchase, the results came back too aggressive. The client was struggling to figure out how to use the data, given that the results were artificially high. Knowing that was a challenge in the past helped us to design a questionnaire and analysis approach that would provide a much more realistic view. (Getting people to realistically report purchase plans is a common challenge in many industries. Some categories are notoriously over-reported, and others are under-reported. An experienced MR professional will be able to advise you of options for dealing with this.)

Hopefully I have made a convincing case that finding existing research will enhance the success of your current project. Now, where will you find it?

FINDING EXISTING RESEARCH

As mentioned earlier, existing information is commonly found through both internal and external sources:

- Industry associations
- Company library/internal website
- Company consultants
- Internal market research department
- Other agencies (ad agency, PR agency)
- Trade magazines

Here are five examples that will help you get started with your search.

1. **Previously funded custom research.** First of all, find out if any primary MR has been sponsored by your company in the last three or four years. You probably do not care about anything older than that because MR has a shelf life. Still, if there has been any recent research done, it is definitely worth looking at the research results and the agency that executed it.

2. **Secondary or off-the-shelf research from MR firms.** In most industries, there is a host of analyst companies and other third-party sources of data. There are also scanner data, data released by large retailers and other third-party sources that could be available for purchase. Sometimes the data available for purchase are in the form of a report that might cost $2,000, or $5,000, or sometimes even $10,000. Other data are available in database form, and you may pay to access slices of the data.

   There are several websites to consult to find out whether or not such research already exists. Research aggregators like *marketresearch.com* and *the-infoshop.com* have databases that you can search.

3. **Data from government sources.** The U.S. Census is a great source of data, and the government makes it publicly available. Also, the fabulous *CIA World Factbook* has details on key facts by country, which is very handy if you are doing global research and need contextual information.

   Wondering how you would apply census data? Here's an example: Let's say you are doing a concept testing study to determine potential adoption of a new home security product. Let's say the product is more concealable than a traditional system, and has some other cool, new features. You are trying to determine what percentage of the market is likely to buy it. For that type of product, you are going to be interested in households that have at least a minimum income level. You probably would not target households with, say, less than $50,000 a year in household income. The first thing you might want to do is simply determine from census data how many households fit in the desired range. Five million? 100 million? Well, the answer is actually about 56 million. Good to know, right?

4. **Your competitors.** Yet another place to look for existing MR is—believe it or not—your competitors. Sometimes companies do MR and then choose to publish some of it. That might be tipping their hand to competitors, but it can also help them fuel a thought leadership campaign. For example, if I work in the transportation industry, I might want to do research on telecommuting trends and publish it so that my clients know that we proactively seek to learn about customer needs. So, yes, I am publishing data that my competitors now have access to, but I am more interested in just making sure my customers know that we are the kind of company that invests in fresh thinking. Surprisingly, then, you might find some very good MR available for free on your competitors' websites (check out the press release sections of their web sites for relevant announcements).

5. **Professional associations.** Another place to find existing, relevant data is with professional associations. Many professional associations fund research, sometimes even on an annual basis, as part of a membership benefits package. Such research is usually featured on association websites and in newsletters.

HIGHLIGHTS

Types of agencies to consider/ Choosing an agency that meets your needs for value add and accountability

Before you hire an MR agency, you need to consider what type of relationship you want to have with that agency. There are a lot of research agencies out there, and some will be a better fit than others in terms of how they work and manage clients. So even if you find, for example, four firms that are technically qualified to do your project, all four are probably not an equal fit.

TYPES OF AGENCIES

Agencies fall along a continuum of "value add." At the extremes, there are staff extension agencies and full-service agencies (see Table 5.1). Of course, many firms fall in between these two points.

TABLE 5.1 TYPES OF AGENCIES

	Staff extension	Full-service
Role	Augments your staff and follows your directions. Lower level of accountability for project success. Often a one- or two-man shop. Or, sometimes an agency that specializes in only the data collection and basic data analysis parts of the process (sometimes called a "field and tab" agency).	True consultancy: Designs methodology, conducts all phases of project execution, delivers recommendations. Ultimate level of accountability for project success.
Value	Basic skills: questionnaire programming, data collection, and data analysis (often cross-tabs).	High-end skills: Advises on optimizing success, provides leadership on all phases, has rich contextual knowledge.
Fees	Lower, and sometimes hourly.	Higher, and often project-based. May include clauses for contingencies.

HOW TO CHOOSE A RELATIONSHIP TYPE

MR agencies vary greatly in the degree to which they truly act as a consulting agency vs. the degree to which they act as more of an extension of your staff. Which would best meet your needs?

A true full-service MR consultancy will be the best fit if you are seeking these types of conditions:

- You'll come to it with objectives, and it will design the research project, getting your approval at key milestone points.

- It will run the show in terms of the details of how to execute the research. It will recommend exactly what methodology to employ.

- It will report the research results and deliver recommendations based on those results.

- It will give you weekly status reports and hold meetings at key junctures to report on status.

With a true, full-service consultancy, you're counting on it to be the professional and contribute the expertise needed to plan, execute, and deliver the research.

Can I Trust an Agency's Recommendation About Methodology?

So you want the research agency to recommend a methodology—and you are entirely open to qualitative, quantitative, or a combination of approaches.

How will the research agency make its recommendation? A respectable agency takes multiple factors into consideration:

- Project objectives
- Geographic scope
- Population parameters
- Audience needs
- Budget parameters
- Timeline parameters

These things can occasionally conflict. I have seen many cases where, in an ideal world, we would take an approach that was optimal for the objectives—but realities of budget and timelines mandated a compromise. It's just reality that sometimes trade-offs need to be made. However, your agency will advise you accordingly when this arises.

It is up to you to state any boundaries you have. If you convey to the agency that budget is more of an issue than time, that will lead to a very different recommendation than a scenario where time is more of an issue than budget.

One note of caution: Some agencies have specific strengths, and tend to see projects accordingly. If you are unsure if you need qualitative or quantitative, be sure to talk to agencies that are equally strong in both so you don't get a skewed view. It's like going to a surgeon for a medical opinion: Everything looks like surgery when you are a surgeon. If you talk only to agencies that are quantitatively oriented, you likely will get a proposal that is weak on qualitative methods.

At the other extreme, there are MR agencies that act more as an extension of your staff. If the following statements are true for you, then you will want a staff extension approach:

- You, the client, are pretty much delegating, on a weekly if not daily basis, exactly what you want and how you want it done.

- You are using it more to execute to your plans, not to contribute substantive research design or methodology expertise.

- You are leading the direction of analysis and interpretation of findings, and will lead the final presentation of results.

- You will not be asking the agency for recommendations based on the research; you and your colleagues will develop them yourselves.

If you have a lot of market research expertise and really just need somebody to augment your staff, this is certainly a fine choice. Remember, though, you get what you pay for. If you hire a firm to act as a staff extension, don't expect it to be a true consultancy. As you search for this type of agency, you should start by looking at data collection firms or "field and tab" houses. There are also many MR freelancers available for this type of work (check out the various professional placement websites, such as *Guru.com*).

Just to be clear: If you hire a staff extension supplier, it is taking orders; it cannot be relied on to push back on you if you're making a poor decision. For example, if you design a questionnaire that isn't clear or has some issues with scales, it won't necessarily recommend alternate suggestions. It will cost a lot less, though, and if you are confident in your expertise, this can be an absolutely fine choice.

HOW TO MANAGE THE CHOSEN RELATIONSHIP TYPE

If you hire a staff augmentation agency, you will need to manage it accordingly. This will be more of a hands-on, daily project management scenario for you. Daily check-ins or status updates are appropriate. You also will need to document your requirements at each phase.

For example, in this scenario you may be designing the questionnaire yourself. Or, you may have the agency design it—but with your significant input. If this is the case, you will need to give clear direction on any preferences you have for questionnaire design. If you know what types of analysis you will want to do at the end of the project, you will need to tell the agency how to design the questionnaire so that you have appropriate data with which to work.

If your organization does not have a full-time research department (or has one and it is fully booked), chances are you will be looking to hire a full-service firm. If you hire a full-service agency, treat it as such. It is a costly mistake to hire a full-service agency, and then treat it like a staff extension. Misery for all involved will surely ensue.

A full-service MR agency is staffed with highly skilled, experienced consultants. If you treat them like a staff extension by micromanaging them, they lose motivation, and you simply will not get the benefit of the expertise for which you are paying.

In addition, if you manage this type of agency as a staff extension, you actually will start to incur extra costs. After all, when the agency originally scoped the project, they assumed you were going to trust its judgment and its recommendations, and any points of disagreement would be resolved in a peer-level discussion. But, for example, if the questionnaire design process takes three times longer than planned because of excessive reviews and an onerous number of unnecessary requests, it's understandable that the agency will start experiencing delays and incurring additional staff time.

It's like an old joke my dad used to tell: A man is driving along one day, and his car breaks down. He has the car towed to the auto shop. The auto mechanic says, "It's going to be $40 an hour for me to fix the car, plus parts." Then the man says, "Well, what if I help?" The auto mechanic doesn't hesitate. He says, "If you help, it'll be $80 an hour."

MANAGING YOUR BUDGET

As you plan to hire a research agency, think about the potential for a broader context: Are you looking for somebody who you can have on call over a long period of time, or somebody with whom you're going to have a very project-oriented, short-term relationship? Do you want the agency to be a consultant on call because of their area of expertise?

If the type of work you need is truly for a particular project or a series of projects, that's how the fee arrangement should be arranged. It will be priced per project.

However, if you have an ongoing need for the agency to be part of your MR process, including ongoing research strategy planning, the type of relationship you are more likely to want is a retainer arrangement.

Full-service agencies often offer retainer options, which provide two important benefits:

1. You can negotiate for guaranteed access to a specific staff member or team for a minimum number of hours per month. Once you have a relationship with a firm, it gets acquainted with your company's unique culture, context, budget sensitivities, and needs. Keeping it on retainer ensures you get access to the right people.

2. A retainer ensures fast response to any time-sensitive questions you might have. Remember that research firms are consultancies—their senior people can be handling two to five projects at a time, if not more. If you don't have a retainer, and call during a period of heavy deadlines, you are unlikely to get a timely or thorough response.

Which of these columns best describes your agency needs?

A	B
Will implement a methodology I specify.	Will give me insightful recommendations about what methodology will best meet our needs.
Will stick to my specifications for sample and quota requirements.	Will have strong recommendations about screening criteria and quotas based on relevant experience.
Will send me raw data as it becomes available.	Will conduct various analyses on the data collected.
Will send me a factual report—with few or no recommendations.	Will write a detailed report, with recommendations.
Will give me the information I need to do a final project presentation to my internal audience and play a secondary role in that meeting (if any at all).	Will credibly present findings to an executive-level audience at our location.

If your preferences lie mostly in column A, you should seek out and send your RFP to data collection firms, or MR freelancers. If your needs are more closely aligned with those in column B, you are seeking a full-service research agency.

HIGHLIGHTS
RFI and RFP content recommendations/ Planning for easy comparisons/ Finding potential agencies

If you want your MR project to precisely meet your goals, you will need a precise RFP. The RFP is necessary to document your research needs and expectations. It also gives you an opportunity to ask for free advice.

Do exceptions exist? Do some clients successfully hire agencies without a formal RFP? Sure. I have clients I have worked with for years, and sometimes they just send me a brief email, send an informal memo, or make a five-minute phone call to convey their needs. These are clients I know—I know what types of research they find most useful, I know what challenges they are likely to face, and I know their typical budget levels. Unless you have a long-standing relationship with an MR agency, I strongly recommend going through an RFP process. It mitigates a lot of risks and ultimately will save you a lot of time.

But I Don't Have Time to Write an RFP!

Taking the time to write an RFP can be problematic, but it's a worthwhile investment for any project over $25,000 (and in the world of custom, primary research—that's most of them). If you don't write an RFP, you will waste much more time on things like the following:

Trying to compare proposals that are based on entirely different assumptions. When all the proposals are based on the same specifications from the same RFP, comparing them is much easier.

Issuing an RFP later because none of the proposals met your expectations. You then have wasted one or two weeks waiting for proposals that were, in effect, useless, and you have to start all over anyway.

Arguing with a research supplier down the road, because it made an assumption that you find objectionable. For example, do you really want to be three weeks into a project only to find out that the supplier's fees were based on the assumption that you were providing the sample? There are many assumptions made in pricing a research study; you really don't want to have to argue about fees once it's underway.

RFP formality varies greatly, depending on the size and scope of your research project. In most cases, it really is fine just to go straight to RFP, to the companies from which you'd like to see proposals. But there are cases when issuing a request for information (RFI) first makes sense. What's the difference?

RFIS

Let's say you're about to do a market segmentation study, and you've identified 10 different companies that all look like potential candidates to meet your needs. You might not want to get 10 actual proposals, because reading and comparing proposals is a very time-consuming process. You might want to add an initial weeding-out phase by sending out an RFI.

The RFI is a form to identify key characteristics of companies in the consideration set, so that you can screen out companies based on important criteria. The goal is to create a manageable short-list of 3 or 4 agencies from the initial larger set (10, in the example above). For example, in the RFI, you might ask in what countries the company has direct offices, or what percent of its work is consumer versus B2B related. That way, if you're only interested in candidates with offices in three specific countries and that does at least 50% consumer work, you can easily thin the herd.

Pssst ... the sneaky thing about an RFI is that it gives you a chance to learn about potential suppliers before tipping your hand as to what you actually want. You can send out an RFI without telling candidates what the ultimate project is about. This way, you are more likely to get an objective profile of their resources and expertise. In contrast, when you send out an RFP for, let's say, a logo testing study, you get a skewed view. Guess what types of responses you will get? Responses that showcase logo testing expertise—even if a little exaggerated.

RFI information is pretty basic. Typically, the RFI asks for information about agency size, history, and areas of specialty. Often, an RFI also requests customer case studies, references, and biographies of key staff members and the executive management team. An example of how common RFI information requests are stated is shown in Table 6-1, along with a description of why each type of information might be important to you. But remember that the content is up to you; just think about it in terms of screening criteria. If you know you will only pick an agency that meets Criterion A, translate that into an RFI question.

TABLE 6.1 COMMON RFI INFORMATION REQUESTS

Common RFI questions	And why you might ask them
List of countries with direct offices	If you are planning a global study, you might prefer an agency that operates in your key markets. This is especially true if localization will be an issue.
Number of full-time equivalents	Is this company primarily relying on subcontractors?
Vertical industry specialties (for B2B)	Some agencies dabble in all industries; others specialize.
Demographic specialties (for consumer research)	Does it specialize in particular segments? For example, some agencies specialize in teens and others in specific ethnic groups.
Methodology specialties	Does it specialize in particular methods? Does it claim a particularly strong skill set in an area of interest to you?
Revenue	You might want to know something about the sales volume, although many agencies are privately held and might not disclose.
Year founded	Has it been around for some time?
Headquarters location	Is it close to you? This is not necessary, but can come in handy for more complex projects.
Links to articles or blogs authored by key employees	Has it published materials that give it relevant credibility? Do you like its style?
Management team list and biographies	Is the company run by researchers? By academics? By business operations professionals? How many have graduate degrees? Do they have backgrounds in your industry? Do their biographies reflect any real passion for research?
Please describe your project management approach	You'll want to get a sense of how seriously it takes this. Does it have a proactive approach? A unique angle? Any online status tools?

What parts of the research process are outsourced or subcontracted? Do you have your own field services facility (data collection call center)?	Some firms outsource a little; others outsource a lot. Translation is commonly outsourced and data analysis less so (especially if you are dealing with a full-service firm).
Does your firm have focus group moderators on staff?	It's not a deal breaker, but some firms do outsource focus group moderation. This can mean that it doesn't do many focus groups. It can also can mean it simply has a network of highly qualified subcontractors. That said, if your project will use focus groups, you might want to consider your direct relationship with the moderator as one of your selection criteria.

The RFI process can be very valuable, but in many cases, it's overkill. The truth of the matter is that you can ask for a lot of the same information in a proposal, so if you're under the gun in terms of schedule, and there are only three firms under consideration anyway, there's nothing wrong with going immediately to RFP.

RFPS

RFPs range widely in terms of their level of sophistication and complexity. If your need is for a simple project, do yourself a favor: keep your RFP simple. It will save you a lot of time when the proposals come back and you actually have to read them.

At minimum, an MR RFP states parameters and requests responses to the basic questions:

- Statement of objectives
- Target population (B2B, B2C)
  - Perhaps with quotas within each sub-target
- Statement of geographic scope
- Sample source: Are you providing it, or is the agency?

- Statement of preference for qualitative or quantitative methodologies, if any

- Deliverables required at project conclusion

- Timeline requirements

- Qualifications required

Figure 6.1 is an example of a simple RFP. The level of brevity in this example is perfectly fine for many projects. Note that the RFP also states when and how to respond. It may seem trivial, but it's important to state that clearly; you don't want agencies making their own assumptions about deadlines or formats.

FIGURE 6.1: SIMPLE RFP FOR A SPECIALTY FOODS MANUFACTURER

Request for Proposal: Specialty Foods Study

RFP Reponses: Please send responses in electronic format to abcde@4321xyz.com no later than November 15, 2009. Only complete responses will be considered.

Objectives: Our goal is to identify customer groups that would be most likely to try a new food bar product with specific flavor characteristics. To do this, we want to measure satisfaction with, and purchase behaviors for, the food bar sector. Which food bars are best liked? Which are liked primarily because of their flavor? Are people loyal to their preferred bars, or are they strongly influenced by price promotions? Are certain flavor and ingredient combinations likely to entice them to try a new bar?

Hypotheses: We believe that brand switching potential varies notably by gender, income, and urban vs. suburban households. We think that interest in specific new flavor and ingredient combinations will vary by gender, age, and activity profiles.

Geographic Scope: This is a U.S. study, although we would like an option to conduct a follow-up phase in Canada.

Sample Source: To be provided by the agency.

Population: We are interested in conducting this research with adults who are physically active (engage in exercise at least three times per week), between the ages of 21 and 65. We want a mix of runners, bikers, rock climbers, skiers, and triathletes.

Methodology: We are open to agency recommendations for methodology, but we have a slight preference for quantitative research because we want some hard numbers as input to our marketing plan.

Deliverables Required: Upon completion, we will want a brief report in Keynote, a complete set of data tables, and an on-site presentation.

Qualifications: Please describe your experience in the specialty foods business that may be relevant. Include the biographies of proposed project staff.

Fee: Please state your fee as a total fee, and with an option for tables only (no slide deck). Also provide a separate option for adding Canada as a Phase 2.

Timeline: Please state your proposed timeline by stage (definition/kickoff, design, data collection, analysis/reporting).

In a more elaborate RFP, you can ask for many things. Table 6.2 shows some suggestions. Not all of these will be relevant to every RFP, but this gives you a good set of options to get you started. If you did use an RFI as a first step, be sure to avoid asking for duplicate information. Want more RFP examples? Check out the website *www.ResearchRockstar.com*.

TABLE 6.2: SUGGESTED ELEMENTS FOR AN RFP

Please provide information about your firm's relevant industry experience.

Provide biographies for the key team members you would assign to this project.

Describe your methodology recommendation and how it will address our objectives.

Provide details of your quality assurance (QA) practices.

How will you ensure sample qualifications?

(For international studies) Please describe your experience collecting data in the target countries.

Please list the critical success factors and risks you see for this project.

Please describe the expected timeline for this project, including key milestones.

Given our objectives, what screening criteria and quotas do you recommend?

(For quantitative studies) What types of data analysis will you conduct?

(For international studies) Please provide pricing as follows: All requested countries; Countries A and B only; Countries A, B, and C only.

How will you keep us informed of project status? In what format and with what frequency? Will I have a dedicated project manager?

Our internal audience requires some education about MR in order to prepare them for the results. How can you address this?

Include at least three examples of report excerpts or visuals (content is understandably confidential, so please provide any sanitized versions available).

Please describe your questionnaire design process.

What project steps will be outsourced?

Is your firm currently engaged with any of our competitors?

Is your agency a member of AAPOR, CASRO, ESOMAR, the MRA or other professional associations?

What deliverables will be included in this project? And in what format?

What type of support do you offer after report delivery?

A NOTE ON LEGALESE

All companies have specific purchasing and contract terms, so be sure to check with your accounting, accounts payable, or legal department for guidelines. Common items in MR RFPs include the following:

- Statement that a nondisclosure agreement (NDA) must be executed prior to engagement.

  - In some cases, you might want an NDA before you even send out an RFP. For example, if you are issuing an RFP that contains proprietary company information because it is key context, you want to execute an NDA first.

- Statement about need for, or process to get, approved vendor status.

- Payment terms. Does your company have a rule that it pays net 45? Or that it only issues checks on the 10th of each month? Do you have a strict process for how all invoices must be submitted? Do you require anything else from the agency before a purchase order can be issued? Tell the agency in case its terms or expectations are different.

These payment process items might seem trivial. But planning for them early on will prevent avoidable delays. Who wants to see an important project delayed two weeks because someone forgot to get the purchase order processed?

SPECIFYING DELIVERABLES

It is always important to precisely state what deliverables you require. Of course, you can always ask the firms responding to your RFP to advise you as to what deliverables they think would be most useful. But if you know what you want, it's in your best interest to say that in the RFP to make sure these deliverables are covered in the fee and timeline estimates that you get back.

For example, let's say you know you will want at least these three items at project conclusion:

1. Five banners of cross-tabs

2. An on-site presentation to an executive-level audience

3. An online reporting tool

All of those things should be stated in the RFP. So, how do you decide what types of deliverables you need?

First, take a moment to think about your internal audience members. Recall how you assessed your audience on these items, back in Chapter 3:

- Receptivity

- Data type preferences

- Sophistication

- Attention span

Keeping that assessment of your audience's unique characteristics in mind, you can also reflect on their reporting preferences. How much interactivity do they like? Are they usually satisfied getting information from a static set of slides (PowerPoint, Keynote, etc.)? Do they like a text document in a more academically written format? Are they an interactive group—will they want a highly interactive presentation or workshop? Will some analytical colleagues want to gets hands-on with the data?

Attention span is also a consideration. Will your audience be willing to spend a few hours delving into the results, or will you be lucky if you get their attention for 30 minutes? Will they only be willing to digest the results during a presentation, or would they also be likely to read and do follow-up?

Figure 6.2 summarizes these considerations. For example, if your audience is primarily people who have a low attention span but do value interactivity, an on-site presentation will be a good match. But if they have a higher attention span, you may find a standard presentation won't be quite enough; they may prefer a workshop where they have more opportunities to get really immersed in the research. Of course, in reality, your audience may be mixed—and you may need to choose one deliverable for one sub-group, and an additional set of deliverables for others.

FIGURE 6.2 MATCHING DELIVERABLES TO AUDIENCE NEEDS

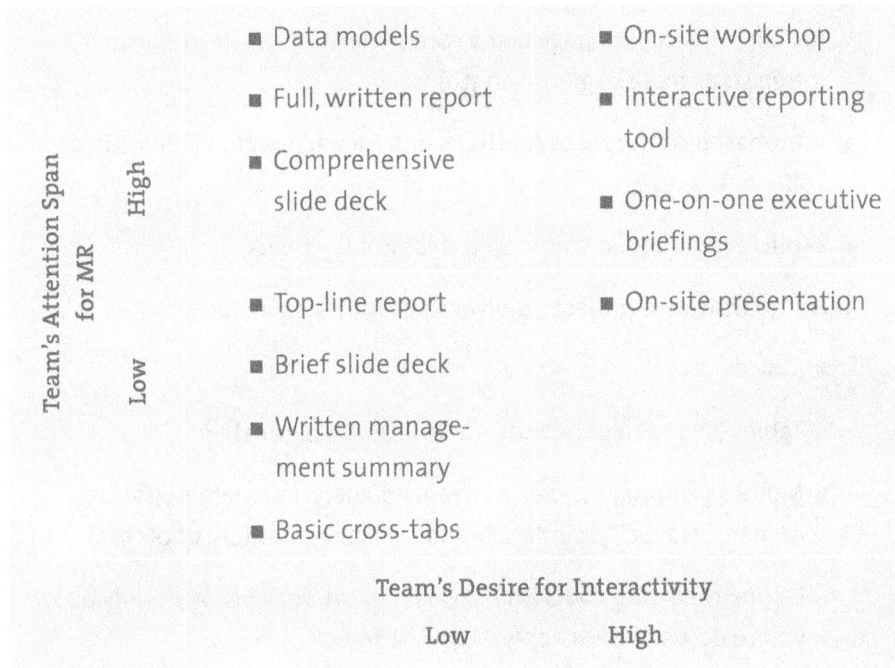

Team's Attention Span for MR		
High	■ Data models ■ Full, written report ■ Comprehensive slide deck	■ On-site workshop ■ Interactive reporting tool ■ One-on-one executive briefings
Low	■ Top-line report ■ Brief slide deck ■ Written management summary ■ Basic cross-tabs	■ On-site presentation
	Low	High
	Team's Desire for Interactivity	

Second, be aware of the many diverse deliverable options. Research project deliverables can include one or more of the following:

- Articles for submission to trade or other professional publications

- Interactive workshop

- On-site presentation (If so, will you need more than one?)

- One-on-one briefings for key executives

- Other meetings (Will you want the researcher to present to your board of directors, investors, channel partners, strategic suppliers?)

- Slide deck (either brief or comprehensive)

- Text document (usually formatted in Word): Written management summary or executive summary

- Text document (usually formatted in Word): Written top-line report (usually less than 10 pages) or a comprehensive, written report (often 50 or more pages in length)

- Web-based conferences (perhaps one for each regional division of your company)

- White papers (most common in technology fields)

- For quantitative projects, deliverables may also include:

  - Raw data

  - Tables (the tables showing all data as cross-tabs)

  - Models (for projects using advanced analytics, there might be demand elasticity models, brand switching models, or others)

  - Online reporting tools (these vary a great deal, but generally allow you to do basic data analysis on the fly)

- For qualitative projects, deliverables may also include:

  - Video of interviews or focus groups, often synthesized to show only the most important parts

  - Audio files

  - Transcripts

Third, consider your budget and timeline needs. Some deliverables obviously cost more and take more time to create. If you are torn, you can always state which deliverables are minimally required and ask for pricing options for others as possible add-ons.

RFP TIPS

Here are some tips of the RFP trade.

Plan ahead for easy comparisons. You want to make sure that the proposals come back in a format that allows you to easily compare and contrast them. Here are two ways to accomplish this:

1. Specify what sections you want, and in what order. For example, write: "In your response, please have separate sections clearly labeled as follows: Pricing, Timeline, Recommended Methods, Recommended Sample plan, Key Assumptions, Criteria for Success."

2. Ask for a table that summarizes key facts from the proposal, such as price and timeline, by phase. You can even create the table in the RFP, so that you get the same table back from all of the bidders. This will make it easier to quickly compare proposals on the most important parameters.

You might be wondering if it is fair to impose proposal format requirements. It certainly is. You're the customer, and you don't have time to compare proposals written and organized in different ways. It's up to the agencies to make sure that they meet your needs.

WHO DO I SEND THIS GREAT RFP TO?

If you need suggestions for how to find potential agencies, here's a list to get you started:

- Past suppliers. Has your firm done custom research in the past? Is there a known agency that has credibility within your company? Is there a list of approved agencies?

- Research directories. *Quirk's* magazine has a directory of research suppliers on its website, as does the New York American Marketing Association (which publishes the well-known *GreenBook*).

- Professional association sites. Check out the listings at CASRO, ESOMAR, and the *Blue Book* from the Marketing Research Association (MRA).

- Colleagues or other business associates. Ask for recommendations from internal clients, colleagues, your ad agency or business-oriented social networks. All of these can be great sources.

Between these sources you should be able to identify at least six or seven candidates. That doesn't mean you should send your RFP to all of them—if necessary, use the RFI prescreening process described earlier. Also, you don't want to get in the habit of sending out RFPs to lots of firms, when you already know you are inclined to one or two. The other agencies will soon learn that you are using them to price check—and they will be less likely to take your next RFP seriously. Proposals take time.

WHAT ABOUT RFQS?

In the MR business, we don't use requests for quotes (RFQs) very often. The RFQ really comes from other industries, like construction and manufacturing, where you're specifying exactly what you want and you're simply looking for a price.

HIGHLIGHTS

How to read and compare proposals/ Checking credentials/ Checking references

Once the RFP responses arrive, then what?

Get comfortable; you have a lot of reading to do!

MR proposals come in many formats and lengths (unless you took the advice given in the previous section and have easily comparable proposals). Some guidelines follow about what you can expect when you get a proposal.

The number of pages indicated in Table 7.1 is for the real content related to your project. Obviously, the larger the project, the longer the proposal will be. In all cases, you can assume an extra five to 20 pages of boilerplate. The boilerplate content includes information about the agency and its credibility proof points (article reprints, magazine quotes, staff biographies, customer case studies, etc).

FIGURE 7.1 TYPICAL PROPOSAL CONTENT

Common Proposal Content	Typical number of pages
Project objectives	Will usually range from 1 to 3 pages, and may include some preliminary hypotheses related to the objectives.
Proposed methodology	Will usually range from 1 to 3 pages. For very large projects, may be specified by phases. For example, there may be a Phase 1 methodology and a Phase 2 methodology.
Proposed sampling plan	Will vary from 1 to 3 pages in most cases, unless there are elaborate quota needs by country.
Suggested approach to analysis	This will vary greatly from 2 to 10 or more pages. If the project requires advanced data analysis, the agencies may include several pages of text describing the proposed approach to analysis and also include images depicting the output of such analyses. This can easily bloat to 10 or more pages.

Proposed deliverables	Will range from 1 to 10 or more pages, especially if the project is A) Mulit-phased or B) Global. In multiphase projects there may be deliverables for each phase. And for global studies, the amount of reporting tends to be very significant, and can even include deliverables for each region.
Project management	3 to 5 pages describing the proposed timeline, project team, and (for larger projects) description of client communications approach.
Fees	Usually 1 to 2 pages, unless it is a very complex, multiphase project, or the client has requested several variations on the pricing. Fees are often specified with payment terms.

One exception is worth noting: The preceding estimates are typical of quantitative research proposals. Qualitative proposals, such as focus group proposals, are often shorter and typically include the following:

- Statement of project objectives

- Explanation of how the focus group guide design can address the objectives

- Details about suggested locations and screening criteria

- Description of deliverables

- Proposed timeline and fees

In any case, you can see that reading proposals is going to take real time. And the bigger the project, the more you will have to read. So plan accordingly.

TIPS FOR READING PROPOSALS

So what should you look for as you read through these proposals? Here are some tips that will help you focus on the most important content.

1. **Avoid comparing solely on price.** When comparing proposals, the temptation is to immediately flip to the last page and compare fee estimates. Is Company A proposing $50,000 and Company B proposing $100,000? Don't dismiss Company B right away—it might simply be using more realistic pricing assumptions.

   As a general rule, if the proposed prices vary by more than 20 percent, you can be certain that the agencies used different assumptions. Pricing will vary if they used different assumptions about the difficulty of finding qualified respondents (also referred to as incidence rate), required deliverables, or the types of data analysis required. Perhaps one agency built in some analyses that would be overkill for you. Perhaps another assumed you were providing the sample and as a result proposed a markedly low fee.

   There's certainly nothing wrong with calling agencies back and redirecting any incorrect assumptions, but why waste the time? If your RFP is precise, you should get fee estimates in the same ballpark. If your RFP is precise, and fees are still really divergent, ask the high and low bidders to comment.

2. **Look at the biographies carefully.** It's always a good idea to compare proposals based on the descriptions of the team bios submitted. A reputable MR firm will tell you something about who's going to be assigned to your project, should it be selected. Read the language carefully: Is it sending you the bios of representative team members or those of the professionals it actually intends to assign?

   Some large MR firms have reputations for bringing in their big guns (senior consultants and VPs) to sell a project, but then relegating actual day-to-day project management to a junior-level person. If your project is simple, you might be better off with more of a junior- to mid-level person because their daily rates are going to be lower, so the research will cost you less. But if you are doing something that's very significant, then you want senior-level project management.

As an aside, the bait-and-switch, when it happens, is often unintentional. If you send out an RFP in January, but don't select a vendor until April, there is a good chance that the initially assigned consultants will be booked with other clients.

Here are a few other things to look for as you review bios:

- Are the bios from full-time employees or subcontractors? Using subcontractors might not be a bad thing, but it does say something about a firm's in-house expertise and ability to handle project loads.

- Do the bios indicate what other clients the team members have worked with? Have they worked with clients in your space? Do they work with your competitors?

  - If they do work with your competitors, don't dismiss them right away. After all, this may mean they have a lot of relevant contextual knowledge from which you can benefit. Of course, you should ask about conflicts of interest and how they would protect your confidential information. One option: simply ask them to not engage with your competitor while they are engaged with you.

- Do the bios show relevant expertise? How many of the proposed team members have worked on similar projects in the past? For example, if you are doing a brand awareness project, what relevant experience is highlighted in the bios?

- How long have team members been with the agency? Have the key members been with the agency for at least three years? That shows that they have a track record with that agency's processes and best practices. After all, if you buy into a sales pitch that includes this firm's approach to, say, project management, you will want someone managing the project that has been applying those project skills for more than a year.

3. **Reality check the proposed timeline.** If one agency is proposing a timeline that is markedly shorter than anybody else's, it's a red flag. Of course, markedly longer is a red flag as well. But in reality, I've seen more clients get burned by agencies that proposed an unrealistically short timeline.

Typically, if one agency's timeline is significantly shorter than everybody else's, it's making overly aggressive promises to win your business. Of course you want the MR data tomorrow, so the promise of a short timeline is enticing. But the truth of the matter is that even in the world of online research (which has quicker data collection than other options), a high-quality primary MR project still takes at least four to six weeks.

Think about it. At minimum, you're going to need two weeks for questionnaire design or moderator guide development alone. And if you have 2 or more internal clients who need to be in on approval cycles or a legal department that has to okay the content, it can easily be more. Rushing through that process is going to cause heartache for everyone at the end of the project. So if a bidding agency proposes a timeline that seems just too good to be true, it probably is. You really need to ask them what their assumptions are for each phase of the project.

Do exceptions exist? Yes. Online or phone surveys can be done in a day or two, provided most of the following conditions are met: if it's a consumer study; if you have a standard questionnaire that you are fielding; if you literally have five or six questions; if you have a great sample source that can execute in 24 hours; if you are buying into an ongoing survey program (referred to as omnibus surveys); and if you don't need any real reporting—just the data.

4. **Review the project management approach.** Compare proposals based on how the firms talk about project management. Do they really seem to understand the importance of managing the project on a day-to-day and week-to-week basis? How do they describe the kickoff process? Do they advocate for in-person kickoffs, or do they seem to prefer a more casual

approach? Do they state that they're going to provide weekly written status memos? How do they say they're going to track key milestones? Are they planning to have weekly status conferences with you, the client? Although the level of project management required varies by project complexity, it's always good to ensure that a potential supplier's approach will align with your expectations.

5. **Look for mentions of QA.** Do they mention QA in their proposals? What kind of process have they built in for doing quality checks throughout the process, not just at the end once the data are collected? What information or best practices do they cite in the proposal that addresses quality at key junctures? If you ask, "What steps do you take to make sure the questionnaire is programmed correctly?" how do they respond? This is a completely valid question. Imagine if you were just done with data collection, only to find that due to a programming error, a key question was displayed with the wrong answer options? Ouch!

6. **Highlight any content that seems odd or wrong.** MR proposals should pass a basic gut check: Does the proposal seem honest and believable? Is the price too good to be true? Are any statements unclear? You should ask about any content you are unsure of.

7. **Beyond boilerplate.** I always prefer a proposal that shows some original thought as opposed to just regurgitating what was in the RFP and adding in some boilerplate. Some MR firms overuse boilerplate. Using boilerplate doesn't mean a proposal is bad, and it doesn't mean the firm is not a good company. But won't you feel better reading a proposal that was clearly written for you, addressing your needs?

8. **Value add (if you are looking for a full service agency).** Look for any evidence that suggests that the MR firm is going to add real value to the project, as opposed to just moving through a process in a robotic fashion. For example, has it identified in the proposal what it thinks the greatest risks are in doing this project successfully and identified what it thinks it can do to mitigate those risks? Has it made it clear that it understands the critical success factors that will make this project successful for you and the rest of your team upon completion? Has it shown that it understands the topic by identifying some preliminary hypotheses that could be relevant to the study? These things show that (a) it cares enough

about the work to really put some thought into the proposal, (b) that it is going to be a partner that is going to add value to the process, and (c) that it really understands your business and will be able to speak credibly with your internal colleagues.

Checking References

Ultimately, part of the proposal review process is calling references. Of course, keep in mind that the references offered in proposals are cherry-picked. Although they can still be valid, it does mean that you have to be a little bit skeptical. I always prefer to check the provided references and seek other unofficial references who can speak to the companies' abilities. Maybe you have a contact who has worked with this firm in the past. Maybe you use a business-specific social networking site that you can leverage to find unofficial references. Many MR firms have a page on their website that lists client names. It is worthwhile to peruse that list in case you happen to know anyone at these companies.

Not sure what to ask during these calls? Here are five questions that will get to the heart of the matter:

- Would you hire this firm again? (Listen for "Yes, but ..." responses.)
- What type of project did it do for you? What methodology was used?
- What could it have done better on your project? (Listen carefully for between-the-lines inferences.)
- What did you think of its final deliverables? (This is where the rubber hits the road on most projects; a firm might do well throughout, but then its reporting or presenters disappoint, which can derail an otherwise well-run project.)
- What did you think of your project manager? (Listen for comments that might help you assess your potential style fit with the firm.)

FOLLOW-UP

The last step of the proposal review process is assessing the degree to which the company has done a good job of following up. Did it just send the RFP response by email and leave it at that? Did it do a good job of following up with phone calls? Did it ask for the opportunity to present its proposal in-person? It's surprising how many MR firms really don't do a good job of following up. Does it really matter? I think so. If it doesn't have time enough to follow up, does it have time for my project? Is this firm resource-constrained?

Responsiveness during follow-up is also a good way to assess potential fit. How somebody responds to your questions during the sales process can be indicative (although not always) of how he or she will respond to your questions should you engage them. A good way to get a sense of the agency's work ethic and client focus is to ask questions after you read its proposal. Now, after you read the proposal you probably will have questions, but if you need a little inspiration, here are some questions that might be relevant:

- What will your sample source be (if not specified clearly)?

- How much time do you suggest for the final presentation, and what is the format you recommend?

- Can you share an example of another project where you (insert relevant example: Gathered data from our specified countries? Did in-depth interviews with recent college grads? Had to provide a focus group moderator well-versed in Web 2.0 topics)?

- How will we collaborate on questionnaire/discussion guide design?

- What challenges do you anticipate? At what key points will we have the greatest risks?

HOW LONG SHOULD I GIVE A MARKET RESEARCH FIRM TO RESPOND TO AN RFP?

The answer to this question varies a lot by an RFP's complexity. At the low end, four to five business days is a minimum. After all, the agency is going to need a day to get the RFP into its pipeline to work on the proposal, and two or three days, even for a basic proposal, to make sure that it puts together the fee estimates and the methodology appropriately.

A large study, say $100,000 or more in size, with a multinational component, is very complex to design and cost out. In that kind of scenario, you need to give an agency at least 10 business days to respond. If you give them less, their response will be rushed—you won't get the best pricing or the most thoughtful recommendations.

WHAT IF I NEED PRICING NOW?

It happens to all of us. Every once in a while, we have an urgent need for MR and we don't have time to go through a formal RFP process. In such cases, there is nothing wrong with calling a few select firms, giving them a broad-brush idea of what you need, and asking them to give you a rough price range for budgeting purposes. In the agency world, we all are asked to do that from time to time, and as long as you set realistic expectations and understand that the pricing could be plus or minus 20 percent, it's absolutely fine to do.

CHECKING CREDENTIALS

The credentials for research professionals vary for qualitative and quantitative methods.

If your project will involve focus groups or in-depth interviews (IDIs), ask about each moderator's qualifications (the moderator is the person who leads the discussions). Anyone who is trained for moderating focus groups is usually also well-prepared for IDIs. I have occasionally worked with people who are strictly IDI interviewers, but that is rare.

Be sure to ask what kind of training moderators have completed. In some cases, people will say, "Oh, yes. They've been certified. They've completed focus group moderator training at either Burke or Riva." Both organizations have high-quality, widely respected focus group moderator training programs.

I do prefer moderators who have had formal training. Some people will admit that their training is on the job, and that doesn't mean that they're going to be bad moderators. But in my experience, the best moderators have had formal training. Unfortunately, a lot of people who are good conversationalists assume that they'd also be good focus group moderators or interviewers, but it takes real skill to be able to do things such as:

- Manage a dominant respondent.

- Stay on topic (avoid the temptation to abandon the client-approved guide).

- Diffuse peer-group competitiveness.

- Understand when you're not getting a truly honest opinion from a passive respondent.

- Get at the "why" behind responses without making participants feel like they're being attacked.

- Keep the momentum going (whether it's a 30-minute IDI or a 2-hour focus group, if the participants are bored, they will not give you great information).

Truly, there are a lot of tricks to the trade.

Also ask if the moderators are on staff or subcontracted. Does it really matter? Not always. Many agencies have regular subcontractors for this function, but if they do subcontract, it's wise to ask questions such as these:

- How many times have you worked with this moderator?

- For what types of projects? (To which you hope they reply with something relevant to your topic.)

- Does he or she have expertise in my industry?

- How many years of experience does he or she have with interviewing or moderation?

- Is his or her experience more with moderating discussions with consumers, or with business professionals?

- What is this person's greatest strength as a moderator or interviewer? (To which you hope they reply: "excellent ability to get past superficial responses," "knows how to probe effectively for the reasons behind specific behaviors and attitudes," or even something like, "keeps participants engaged during the process. Keeps energy levels high"; those would all be comforting things to hear).

QUANTITATIVE CREDENTIALS

If you're doing quantitative work, you need to know something about the qualifications of the people who are going to be doing the statistical analysis. You also need to know how much of the quantitative process is handled in-house vs. outsourced.

Some research agencies do outsource statistical analysis tasks (although any shop that has 10 or more employees will at least handle basic statistics in-house: descriptives, cross-tabs, etc.). Outsourcing can be fine, especially in the following scenarios:

- You want an agency that has deep expertise in your industry. Let's say you are in the pharmaceutical industry, where a lot of industry expertise is required to design a meaningful project and analyze the findings with the right context. In this case, you might be fine with a firm that outsources the higher-end statistical analysis because it simply isn't possible to find an agency that has both sets of deep expertise in-house.

- You have purposely decided to work with a smaller agency (a perfectly legitimate choice). Some smaller agencies stay small by using a network of trusted partners for handling overload times and less frequently required skills.

It's also important to understand a firm's comfort with statistical analyses, even if it does outsource them. What types of quantitative techniques has it used? At the low-end extreme, it might simply be generating frequencies and cross-tabs. For some projects, that is absolutely fine. But if you are doing a project in which you are trying to forecast behaviors, segment a market, or otherwise model customer attitudes—projects that have some sort of predictive aspect—then you need a firm with more robust analytic skills. Here are some techniques to listen for:

- Numerous types of multiple regression including linear, non-linear, logistic, and multinomial logistic regression

- Tradeoff analyses, including Conjoint, Discrete Choice, and related hybrid designs

- Factor Analysis and Principal Components Analysis (PCA)

- Latent class modeling

- Decision tree analytics including CHAID and Exhaustive CHAID

- Hierarchical Bayes modeling

If an agency informs you it routinely applies these methods, it probably keeps up with the current state of quantitative methods. Alas, this is important: I have run into MR firms in the past that insist they can handle quantitative work, but when I ask them questions like "What techniques do you apply in segmentation studies?" their answers reveal that in reality, they are not well-versed in the currently available set of analytic tools to perform such projects with excellence.

PROFESSIONAL ASSOCIATIONS

A truly reputable market research company that follows best-in-class practices will most likely be a member of at least one of these professional associations: AAPOR, CASRO, ESOMAR, or the MRA. Here's a hint: **if a firm has never even heard of these associations, buyer beware!**

- The American Association for Public Opinion Research (AAPOR) is a U.S.-based organization of public opinion and survey research professionals. Its members include professionals from academia, government, media, non-profits, and private industry. APPOR provides various materials and educational resources on its website and also publishes *Public Opinion Quarterly*.

- CASRO does a lot of work for the MR industry in terms of establishing best practices for conducting MR and for managing the industry's relationship with people who actually take surveys. For example, there's a Code of Standards and Ethics for Survey Research that CASRO member organizations agree to abide by, which is quite important: It helps make sure that the MR industry maintains a high level of credibility. Credibility is crucial, so that when people are asked to take surveys, they're comfortable complying with our requests to participate.

- ESOMAR is a 5,000+ member international organization that promotes the role of market research and related best practices. It also publishes *Research World*, and hosts events for MR professionals.

- Professional MR organizations are also often members of the MRA. Also, as mentioned in Chapter 6, the MRA publishes an annual directory, the *Blue Book*, which is available online. The *Blue Book* lists MR providers by location and areas of specialty. The MRA is more U.S.-centric (as compared to ESOMAR), and hosts various conferences and events.

If you find yourself evaluating firms that don't belong to at least one of these organizations, I would ask them why they don't. This is a good way just to make sure that you're talking with somebody who isn't just claiming to do MR, but somebody who really is a professional practitioner.

PUBLICATIONS

Have the MR firm's executives or project managers had articles published in magazines such as *Quirk's*, the *Journal of Marketing Research* or *Marketing News* (an AMA publication)? Authoring articles lends some credibility to a company.

That said, smaller MR agencies often don't have time to author articles, let alone go through the tedious process of placing them. Don't let a lack of publications prohibit you from choosing a company. But if the firm has published, it can give you some insight into its areas of expertise and provide evidence to back up any claims it might have about a particular area of expertise.

SPEAKING ENGAGEMENTS

MR agencies often will send their executives to present at conferences hosted by the MRA, ESOMAR, and other professional groups. This can be a great way to meet agency representatives with the pressure of being in a current sales process. However, smaller agencies don't always have the resources to participate in such events.

CHOOSING YOUR AGENCY FROM A SHORT LIST

Once you have narrowed your list to two or three firms, what's next? You will probably have a strong feel based on personality fit, but if you are truly conflicted, here are two approaches you can use to break the tie:

APPROACH A

Pick a tie-breaker criterion, and be objective. In my experience, too many people use price. Price is important, but take a moment to really reflect. Isn't there some criterion that is even more important to you? Which finalist would be best at the following tasks:

- Delivering results with credibility to your executive management team?

- Getting along with your project team?

- Adding value to the process through relevant contextual knowledge?

- Keeping your project true to stated objectives through a formal project management approach?

- Having enough business savvy to accurately interpret results and help drive real business decisions?

Assuming that the finalists are all equivalently attractive based on methodology and deliverables, it could be one of the "softer" items such as these that turn out to be the most useful tie-breaker.

APPROACH B

Create a weighted scorecard. If you really don't have one criterion you can objectively use as a tie-breaker, pick your top five to seven items and create a scorecard. A weighted scorecard, like the one shown in Figure 7.1, helps to keep you honest about what is really important in your selection process.

Set your weights such that they total 100 points. In this example, the client values presentation skills above other items, because in this case, the project's success will primarily be judged by how well the agency delivers the key findings to the management team. In other cases, a client might value other items more.

To create the scorecard, follow these steps:

STEP 1: Identify your criteria (it's best to keep it simple, with five to seven items at most).

STEP 2: Assign weights, such that they add to 100. Is timeline commitment twice as important as fee to you? Then you might assign timeline at 20 and fee at 10, as in this example.

STEP 3: Assess your finalists on each item, using a scale of 1 to 5. In this scale, 1 means "weakness" and 5 means "strength." A neutral score is 3. In this example, Agency A has okay fees (a 3), and Agency Z has very attractive fees (rated a 5).

STEP 4: Tally the results, and make your decision.

FIGURE 7.2 A WEIGHTED SCORECARD

Criteria	Weight	Agency A		Agency Z	
Fee	10	3	30	5	50
Insight into project objectives	10	5	50	3	30
Presentation skills	30	4	120	2	60
References	10	4	40	3	30
Relationship style fit	20	5	100	4	80
Timeline commitment	20	2	40	5	100
TOTAL	**100**		**380**		**350**

Defining roles and responsibilities/ Identifying legitimate red flags/ Judging success

You have hired an agency. Congratulations! Now what?

First, define your internal team. If the project is fairly small, one person can easily handle all the tasks. For larger projects, think about assigning roles for the following functions, although one person can certainly have more than one role:

- DAILY CONTACT: The person who will be the agency's daily contact for questions and approvals, facilitate contract details, and also coordinate any conference calls or on-site meetings.

- SENIOR PROJECT MANAGER: The person who has approval authority for questionnaire or discussion guide designs. This person also will approve any presentation materials prior to the final presentation (if applicable).

- CONTENT EXPERT: At least one person should be assigned to provide the agency with access to the following:

  - Previous research

  - In-depth industry expertise

Client-side project management plays a critical role in project success. A good client-side project team can have a huge impact on overall project outcome. Yes, the agency is doing its "work," but there are several points where your involvement will make it—and ultimately the entire project—successful (see Table 8.1).

TABLE 8.1 A CLIENT ROLES AND RESPONSIBILITIES

Project stage	Client roles and responsibilities
Definition	Define objectives, participate in hypothesis development, approve content priorities. Coordinate internal team as needed to get buy-in on these items. Get agreement from internal clients on success criteria.
Kickoff	Obtain contract approvals, PO numbers, and any other accounting or legal requirements.
Design	Approve and provide feedback on research instrument drafts and sampling plans. Coordinate internal feedback and approval as needed. Manage potential in-house research vampires.
Data collection	Quantitative: Review progress reports; make sure you are comfortable with the quotas and how they are being met. Qualitative: Review progress reports; if IDIs, listen to first three to five as a QA check. You can either listen in real-time or request audio files. I prefer audio files—it gives you the flexibility to listen at your convenience, and to replay as needed. If focus groups, you should attend.
Reporting	Even if the agency is writing the report, the client still has a role. You can ask to review the report outline before the report is started (or, you can choose to entirely trust it, and that's certainly fine, but it is often best to get a heads up in case it is taking the report in a direction that you know will be hard for your internal clients to digest). Provide any templates to which you require adherence. If this is applicable, be sure to provide these early in the process—otherwise you might experience delays if it has to apply your templates after it has already started report development.

Final presentation	Coordinate meeting facilities and attendees. Advise the agency you will want to see a draft of the presentation three to five business days prior to the meeting (if applicable). Arrange for an executive endorser to be present at the meeting. Prepare the endorser to make sure she or he is ready to make a statement about why the research is important and how the team members should seek to apply it.
Throughout	Keep internal clients informed and set realistic expectations. As needed, and this varies by company, keep internal clients updated on schedule, content, and other expectations. In many companies, this is done biweekly, but in others internal clients are only updated at key milestones.
Post-project	That's right; you are not done, even if the agency is. Upon project conclusion, your key tasks are the following: ■ Gather feedback from internal clients and colleagues. ■ Provide feedback to the agency. ■ Post reports or other deliverables on servers, in corporate libraries, etc. ■ Complete internal requests, which may include audience-specific reports, one-off requests for charts, or options for follow-on research. ■ Celebrate!

ESCALATION PROCESS

It is also a good idea to have a preplanned escalation process. In the event that the project has any challenges, you'll want to have a clearly defined plan as to how and to whom to escalate. For example, if the data collection process experiences significant challenges such that some quotas won't be met, who in your organization needs to know? Who will need to approve a fallback plan for substitute quotas? Having some plans for this ahead of time will ensure that any obstacles can be swiftly overcome. Similarly, you should ask the agency what its escalation process is. In the event you are not happy with progress, to whom in its organization can you escalate?

WORKING WITH THE AGENCY AT PROJECT INITIATION

Once you select an agency, a few things will happen, likely in this order:

- **The kickoff meeting.** First, the agency will set up a kickoff meeting. For projects under $50,000, this could easily be done by conference call or Web conference. For larger projects, the kickoff is usually done in-person. At the kickoff meeting, you can expect an agenda similar to that in Table 8.2.

  - What about videoconferencing? If your organization has the facility and is comfortable with it, great! Some agencies have group video-conferencing systems or access to them. As long as the conference can be set up for group viewing (as opposed to just a "talking head" on individual PCs), and preferably has whiteboarding, it can work.

- **Project schedule.** After the kickoff meeting, the agency will deliver a schedule with target milestone dates. This schedule will also usually specify dependencies, such as what milestones require your involvement. After all, the agency cannot stay on schedule during question-naire design, for example, if your team is on vacation that week and unavailable to provide feedback or the necessary approvals.

- It is important that you carefully review this schedule and approve it. If you feel some dates are overly aggressively or oddly lax, ask about it. Also, be sure to watch for potential schedule conflicts. Is the target date for the final presentation in conflict with a major company event on your side? If so, you might want to request a change—you don't want your internal colleagues distracted when the results come in.

- **Work begins.** At this point, the agency starts the real work of designing a questionnaire or discussion guide, and finalizing sample criteria such that lists can be ordered.

- **Weekly status reports or project team meetings begin.** Weekly status updates will be delivered using some combination of the following methods:

  - Weekly written memos

  - Updates to a shared, online project calendar

  - Weekly status calls

TABLE 8.2 SAMPLE KICKOFF MEETING AGENDA

Agenda item	Description
Introductions	Agency and client introductions of key team members; individual roles are explained.
Review of objectives and hypotheses	These three parts might seem redundant with the proposal. They are. However, it is always wise to reiterate the key project parameters live to ensure complete agreement.
Review of methodology	
Discussion of sampling plan	
Success criteria statement and other client-side requirements	Be clear with the agency by using the kickoff meeting to state and document your success criteria. "We will consider this project a success if at the end, we ...." Advise the agency of any special requirements such as adhering to slide templates, using logo treatments, and who should and should not be copied on memos.
Examples or samples from relevant studies	Agencies will often show some examples of end deliverables from similar projects to start to gather feedback and set expectations for the final reporting format, content, and style.
Research content brainstorming	If applicable, the agency may use the kickoff meeting to facilitate some brainstorming about key hypotheses.

MANAGING THE AGENCY DURING THE PROJECT

Now that the project is underway, and your budget is deeply invested, you will be very sensitive to any signs of trouble. That's fine, but understand that custom research is complex. It's important to stay calm and assess situations rationally. Still, sometimes things will happen and you will wonder, "Is this a problem? Should I escalate?" Some examples and guidelines are shown in Table 8.3.

TABLE 8.3 DETERMINING RED FLAGS

Red flag?	Legitimate concern?
Questionnaire design process is behind schedule by more than two days	NO: Not if your team has been changing direction about priorities and scope during the design process. YES: If you, the client, has stayed true to original objectives and your hypotheses were clearly laid out. A delay in this case might indicate the agency is overbooked.
Questionnaire drafts are coming in with seemingly irrelevant content or poor construction	NO: Not if the agency is using a specific indirect method. For example, there are certain ways of constructing questions such that the most objective data can be gathered. Sometimes it might seem indirect—but there is a reason. For example, let's take the example of a project on brand preferences. Instead of asking people what they think of Brand X, we might ask what they think of Brands X, Y, and Z. Do we care about Y and Z? Maybe not. But we don't want to tip our hand to the participant that we do care about X. This is a simple example, but hopefully demonstrates why you might find a question off point. It might, in fact, be a good choice. YES: If the draft reveals a clear lack of understanding about the topic, ask about it. If you feel that a survey taker would find the flow confusing, ask about it. If brand names are misspelled or other sloppy work is evident, escalate it.
Data collection process is behind schedule by more than three days	NO: Not a real red flag if a legitimate roadblock has come up. Examples of common, legitimate issues: (a) you provided your own list, and it is not performing well; (b) you are collecting data in a country that is experiencing a political event, labor strike, national holiday, or other disruptive event. YES: If the agency had at least a week prior to data collection beginning with your approval on screening criteria and quotas, this could be a legitimate red flag. Ask about it. There could be a valid explanation, but it is worth asking.

At a midpoint progress meeting, you feel the project team is unprepared or distracted	**POSSIBLE:** This can be a very legitimate red flag. Are they showing up to important meetings ill-prepared? Unable to answer questions on the fly? That suggests they are overbooked. If you feel that the resources assigned to your project are not being given adequate time, escalate it. It is perfectly fine to remind the agency that you hired it with the understanding that it would adequately staff your project—and that you now feel this is not happening.
You find errors or suspicious data in a memo or report	**POSSIBLE:** If you find any data suspicious at all, ask about it immediately. Most likely, the data were not labeled clearly (such that you were unable to interpret correctly). Professional research firms have QA processes that really do minimize the chance of data errors. Still, it happens, and if you feel at all uncomfortable or suspicious about data you see, you should immediately identify the specific data points and calmly ask for clarification. Don't risk antagonizing the hard-working researcher by over-reacting; chances are, there is a logical explanation.
The agency is unable to send you a draft of the final presentation three days prior to the in-person presentation of findings	**VERY LIKELY.** If your project includes a final presentation upon conclusion, the agency will have been working on it for at least a week prior to delivery, and more likely for two weeks (especially for large projects). Will it be 100 percent complete three days before the presentation? Not necessarily, but it should be at least 80 percent complete. Very often, the last few days are spent polishing and editing, so the agency should at least be able to send you the management summary or some subsections. And you should ask for it. The last thing you want is to find out—too late—that the agency rushed to pull together a haphazard presentation. Let it know you will want to see it at least three days before, and it should be able to comply. If it can't comply, escalate the issue. An experienced researcher will not expect to reveal a research study's results to your internal clients without having given you ample opportunity to preview it. An important exception: If you have given the agency a very short deadline, it may be unreasonable to ask for a preview of more than a day in advance. Don't ask them to generate a final presentation in less than five business days and expect a preview two days later.

In all of these cases, an important premise is that you and your agency are working together towards a common goal: the project's ultimate success. So even if you do see legitimate red flags, the best approach is to be reasonable; ask for an explanation, and ask for options to resolve the problem. Even if the agency did make a mistake—and it does happen—there will likely be very viable solutions.

HIGHLIGHTS

Planning for Retention/ Delivering an engaging presentation/ Creative deliverables

Back in Table 3.1, we talked about how to assess your internal audience's readiness for research. Four parameters were referenced:

1. Receptivity

2. Data type preferences

3. Sophistication

4. Attention span

Later, in Chapter 6, we talked about using a map of attention span and desire for interactivity as a way to choose the best deliverables (recall Figure 6.2, Matching Deliverables to Audience Needs). So by now, you know how to A) design a project that will be aligned with your audience's needs and B) select deliverables that will be most appropriate. Great! Now let's turn our attention to how to make sure those deliverables really have impact at project completion.

PLANNING FOR RETENTION

As we consider the audience's needs, bear in mind learnings from the education and training sectors. Sharing MR results is essentially training people to apply new information. What lessons from these other sectors can we apply?

- **Repetition is important.** Just like when we're teaching kids how to spell, practice makes perfect. The first time people hear information it has a certain amount of impact, but if they hear that information two or three times it improves retention.

- **Multiple modes are important.** We're more likely to retain information if we read it, hear it, and see it in visual displays like graphs and charts. Better still, if we get to apply it through practice quizzes, role-playing, or other interactive exercise. In contrast, if we only read something, we retain far less.

What does this mean? It means **we can't just email out a research report and assume the project has now been delivered.** If we expect people to retain and apply research results, we have to create a more comprehensive delivery strategy.

SLIDE DECKS: NOT JUST OVERUSED, ABUSED

A lot has been written in recent years about how slideware is overused. Well, it is overused. I don't think anybody would disagree with that, but it's still a very efficient way of delivering MR results. And it is likely that it was one of the deliverables you selected for your project.

So let's use it, without abusing it. We've all seen MR reports that were basically 300 pages of poorly labeled charts with very little helpful text. Who's going to get anything useful out of such a report? Those reports are created too often, and they're not very helpful.

Let's stop blaming the slideware, and start using it sensibly. Let's start with the basics.

- **Keep the MR report very modular** so that the executive summary or the management summary, as you prefer, can be a stand-alone document of no more than 10 slides that would give an executive audience everything they really need as key takeaways. Now if they want the supporting details, obviously they can refer to the main body of the report.

- **Organize the report by project objective.** Avoid writing (or if you are using an agency, approving) a report that shows the results by order of question as appeared in the questionnaire. That approach shows that nobody is really thinking about the logical use of the data. Instead, it is usually best to have reports organized by logical objective. This way, if there are three or four objectives covered by the study, a reader who's only interested in one or two can get the relevant information easily without slogging through 240 unnecessary pages.

ROLES AT THE PRESENTATION

Finally! After all of your hard work, the findings are ready to be presented. This is your opportunity to make sure the research will have real impact. Preparing an excellent presentation experience—not just a great slide deck—can be critical to the success of your project.

To some extent, you will have to act as a stage manager, deciding who stands or sits where, who queues whom, and so on. Like any good performance, the roles need to be defined and assigned. Of course, depending on the scope of the presentation, one person can handle multiple roles. Also, the agency can handle some roles (if you are using a full-service agency), but I strongly suggest you make this perfectly clear ahead of time, and assign the following roles:

- **Context provider.** Someone must be prepared to serve as the project's salesman. Why are we here? What prompted us to spend real money for this research? Why should anyone care?

- **Executive endorser.** Presentations, especially those that may have controversial findings, need an executive endorser present to show that (a) the results are important enough that even he or she is in attendance, and (b) there is an expectation that the research will be used.

  - This role gets completely squandered if an executive comes in, makes an opening statement, and then leaves to attend to something "more pressing." Make sure your endorser is committed to stay for the meeting.

- **Research design expert.** Someone needs to have project details memorized and relevant documents handy. This includes familiarity with the questionnaire or discussion guide. If an audience member asks how Question 23 was worded, you must able to answer immediately. Other likely questions will come up around sample source, sample size, quota distributions, and data collection timing (how fresh is this data?).

- **Scribe.** One person should be responsible for taking notes, documening questions, and keeping a list of follow-up actions.

- **Timekeeper**. If some of your most important points are in the second half of your presentation, you need a timekeeper to make sure you get there.

ENGAGING THE AUDIENCE

As with any presentation, the last thing you want to do is have someone read the slides out loud. Boring. Instead, use these tips to avoid the standard reading of slides.

1. **Be sure that there are opportunities for people to participate, especially if the presentation is going to be more than 40 minutes long.** No matter how fascinated you think the audience members should be, most people lose interest after 40 minutes. Give them an opportunity to participate by having a Q&A break or actually be involved in doing exercises.

   - What type of exercise? Let's say you're doing an MR study on market segmentation, and you've just presented three customer groups that have been identified by the research as having varying levels of interest in the product category in question, and having different types of behaviors and characteristics based on demographics, hobbies, psychographics, and so forth. You could stop in the middle of your presentation and ask people, given what they've heard so far, to jot down ideas for naming those segments. It's often helpful to infuse a little humor and encourage people that there are no wrong answers. The crazier the better, because often a memorable segment name will actually be used more than a boring descriptive name would. Have a few people share their names, and you'll likely find an interesting conversation develops. That's just one example of something that can be done in the middle of a presentation to give people a break from hearing someone drone on and get them involved in applying what they've just heard.

2. **Ask your MR supplier to infuse examples of other customers into the presentation.** So, for example, if it is doing a presentation on product concept testing and it's had a particular type of unexpected result, it should—if it's a company that's been around for a while—be able to talk about other cases with similar types of results and how the client chose to use the research, validate the research, or otherwise take action based on the results. Actually being able to talk about real case studies during the presentation can bring it to life for people, and make it sound a lot less academic.

3. **Stop and ask for feedback.** A good way to keep people alert is to stop from time to time and ask questions. "Is this result surprising to you? How do you think you could use it?" Also, if appropriate, you can ask: "Is this result something we could share with our customers? Might they find it interesting? Is it something we could share with our channel partners? Could it help them understand our market better?"

4. **Don't be shy.** If I have an audience member who looks grumpy, I ask, "It seems like you might be uncomfortable with some of these results. Do you have any questions or concerns I can help with?" Usually it's because he or she is not really mentally present. Letting this person know you will put him or her on the spot will get attention.

5. **Ask for the audience's help.** I will sometimes display a chart, share my interpretation of its implications, and then ask, "How about the rest of you? Do you have a different interpretation of this finding?" or, "I was surprised at this finding. Do any of you have any experiences that might shed light on why so many customers think this about us?" Engaging the audience lends credibility and energy.

PRESENTATION TACTICS: Q & A

Q: Should you send the presentation out ahead of time? Or should the big reveal be at the presentation?

A: This depends on your audience. In some companies, if you send the deck to executives ahead of time, they might decide that they no longer need to come to the meeting. This is unfortunate, because the meeting— although certainly vying for their limited time—is the best way for them to become truly immersed in the results. One option is to send only a subset of the slides as a teaser—perhaps the first five slides of the management summary, or perhaps a few slides of particularly juicy results.

If your presentation will be attended by more hands-on or technical people, it is often best to send the deck out ahead of time. This type of audience likes to come prepared with their questions so that they can get the most out of the in-person time.

Q: Should you give out hard copies at the presentation?

A: Yes. In my experience, many people prefer to take notes of interest on the slides so that they don't end up with two separate hard-copy documents (handwritten notes on notebook paper and a slide deck). Also, they might hear the presenter add a verbal anecdote while explaining a slide and decide to note it themselves on the hard copy (after all, not every interesting observation made by a presenter is captured in slide text).

Q: Should questions be saved until the end of the meeting?

A: No. If people have relevant questions early on and they don't get the answers, it really distracts from their experience—and can even lead to perceived lack of credibility. If a presenter holds off an audience member's question, it suggests that he or she so easily distracted that even a single question will derail the presentation. Answering questions as they occur keeps things lively and interactive, and it also boosts perceived credibility.

SLIDEWARE ALTERNATIVES

Instead of delivering a big slideware presentation, consider delivering the research in the form of newsletters. This is especially useful if your audience isn't going to spend more than five minutes at a time reading research results.

In fact, in some cases I've actually broken research results down into logical topics that can be covered in a newsletter-style format, or a word processing document that has two columns per page, rather than having full-page charts and graphs and big blocks of text. Newsletter graphics are smaller, and by restricting the overall document to three to seven pages, you're giving people information in bite-sized chunks that are a lot easier for them to chew and swallow. Although you and I might like reading large MR reports, most people, alas, find them hard to read.

Another option for delivery is video. Some companies have the researcher present the research results on video, in addition to an in-person presentation. The video can be set up so that the display switches back and forth between shots of a person presenting and shots of the slides. The client posts this material on its internal network so that people can watch the presentation at their leisure. On occasion, companies actually put the material on a publically accessible website so that customers also can view the research results. That has the added benefit of creating a piece of thought leadership.

What About Podcasts?

Yes! Audio is a great way to share research results. Keep in mind these pointers:

- 15-20 minutes maximum duration. As many podcasters know, most people have a limited attention span for audio-only formats.
- Use the podcast as an opportunity to advertise executive endorsement. Rather than just read results, include an interview with an executive about what he or she found most interesting about the research. This keeps the content more engaging for listeners.
- Don't forget to use this as a commercial: Close with directions on where to get the full results or how to ask for follow-up.

ASSESSING PROJECT SUCCESS

So what makes an MR study a success or a failure? If at project conclusion the following criteria are met, it was a success. If not, some degree of failure must be acknowledged—and if possible—remedied:

1. Project completed on time.

2. Project completed on budget.

3. Project results clearly align with defined project objectives.

4. Sample size and quota distributions met.

5. Reporting and deliverables meet professional standards.

6. Ethics standards were adhered to.

7. Research results are deemed credible and actionable by clients (whether to inform strategies, make decisions, or otherwise improve the business).

8. Research supplier provided meaningful recommendations and interpretations (assuming you hired a full-service agency).

CELEBRATE!

There is nothing like a little fun and humor to conclude a successful project! T-shirts, posters, mugs, and other items can be easily designed in-house, or purchased at online customization sites. A small gift at the final presentation can serve as a pleasant reminder of the project, leaving a positive impression that will make it easier when seeking budget for your next project.

Appendix A: Some Jargon

The MR industry has its fair share of jargon. Familiarity with these phrases will make your life easier as you start to develop research plans and engage in discussions with agencies.

FOCUS GROUP

A focus group is a research event where a group of eight to 10 participants join in a discussion facilitated by a professional focus group moderator. The groups are held at focus group facilities, which are set up with one-way mirrors and recording devices. In some cases, smaller groups—even dyads or triads—are used to reach a balance between the variety of input from a focus group and the depth of a 1:1 interview.

IDI

In-depth Interviews (IDIs) are commonly used in both consumer and B2B research. Usually lasting 15 minutes to one hour, these one-on-one research events are conducted either by phone, at the respondents' locations, or in a focus group facility (so that the interview can be taped).

INSTRUMENT

The term "instrument" refers to any designed document used for collecting data (a questionnaire is an instrument) or guiding a qualitative discussion (a focus group discussion guide used by the moderator is also an instrument).

PRIMARY RESEARCH

Primary research is original research—as opposed to a summary of pre-published sources. It involves collecting data either though observation (such as taking the temperature every day over 10 years to look at trends) or data collection techniques such as quantitative or qualitative methods. If you hire a market research agency to do a survey project, you are doing primary research.

QUALITATIVE RESEARCH

Qualitative research is often used as a Phase 1—occurring prior to a quantitative Phase 2. Qualitative research provides an opportunity to discover items (behaviors, attitudes, values) that then can be measured in a quantitative study. It also can be used to determine if quantitative research is warranted; that is, by gathering information in a qualitative project, the researcher may determine if a quantitative follow-up is necessary. Still, there are many cases where qualitative research in itself is the methodology for an entire project.

Qualitative research, usually in the form of focus groups, in-depth interviews, or online discussion boards, is a popular choice for topics where body language and facial expression responses are useful. Thus, it is often a popular choice for ad/logo testing, package testing, and other creative topics.

In reality, qualitative research is also often done when budgets are not available for a larger-scale, quantitative approach. Given the options of no research and conducting a handful of qualitative interviews, well, the choice is obvious.

Qualitative methods are also an excellent way to "peel the onion" behind measured behaviors or attitudes. For example, perhaps you discover that only 30 percent of your customer base is using a feature of your newest software product—qualitative research would be a great way to learn why more customers are not doing so.

QUANTITATIVE RESEARCH

Quantitative research involves collecting large amounts of data in order to test specific hypotheses or measure specific items (such as behaviors or attitudes). The process of quantitative research typically includes collecting data from hundreds or thousands of people (or organizations, government agencies, or other entities). By collecting large enough data sets, the researcher can draw conclusions about how the data represents an entre population. For example, a survey of 500 small-business owners about their challenges with cash flow management can be designed such that it is representative of all small businesses. At the end of the project, the researcher can make some hard statements about what percent of small business, perhaps, are seeking large credit lines to help manage cash flow.

When starting a quantitative project, the researcher typically has very specific hypotheses to test or questions to answer. Quantitative is not appropriate for discovery—that's what qualitative research is for.

SAMPLE

Sample refers to the people who are participating in the research—completing a questionnaire, or being recruited to participate in a focus group or an interview. That is, the "sample" is the group of people representing the broader population. If you want to do research among people who buy crossover vehicles, you may want a sample that is defined as people who either own them or plan to buy them in the next six months. You may choose to further define your sample based on income range (perhaps you only want to gather information from people who earn more than $50,000 a year), or a specific gender mix.

SECONDARY RESEARCH

Secondary research is pre-published by someone or some firm other than you. Typically, this research costs money to acquire. It is typically based on information from previously conducted studies. Examples of secondary research include Census Bureau data, encyclopedias, articles in newsletters, and analyst reports.

SYNDICATED RESEARCH

Some research firms offer syndicated research services to their clients. In such a service, the research firm designs and executes the research—and then makes the results available to its paying customers. In some cases, these are multi-client studies—where a group of clients with similar interests collaborate on a research design, share the costs, and share the results.

For more MR jargon, there are great glossaries available online from Quirk's Market Research Review website, and the Marketing Research Association's website.

ABOUT THE AUTHOR

Kathryn Korostoff is a successful entrepreneur and market research professional with a special interest in how organizations acquire, manage, and apply market research. Over the past 20 years, she has personally directed more than 600 primary market research projects and published over 100 bylined articles in trade magazines.

Currently, Kathryn spends her time assisting companies as they create market research departments, develop market research strategies, or otherwise optimize their use of market research. She is also the founder and president of Research RockStar, a company that delivers online How-To's and Best Practices to professionals seeking to get the most from their market research investments. Prior to Research RockStar, Kathryn completed the transition of Sage Research—an agency that she founded and led for 13 years—to its new parent company.

Kathryn serves on the Board of Directors of The Genesis Fund (a non-profit) and the Entrepreneurs' Organization, Boston Chapter. She holds an MBA from Boston University and a BA from Hampshire College.

For further information, please visit ResearchRockStar.com.

STORIES WANTED!

I want to hear your market research stories.

Do you have tales of market research woe? Or market research success?

Has this book helped you meet your market research goals?

Please email any stories or anecdotes to: *kkorostoff@researchrockstar.com*